# ULTIMATE ENERGY
## How To Get From Tired To Inspired

# ULTIMATE ENERGY

## How To Get From Tired To Inspired

• • • • • •

TRICIA WOOLFREY

*British Library Cataloguing in Publication Data*: a catalogue record for this title is available from the British Library.

*Library of Congress Catalog Card Number*: on file.

ISBN: 9781473634732
eISBN: 9781473634756

1

Designed and set by Craig Burgess
Cover image © Shutterstock.com
Printed and bound in Great Britain by CPI Group (UK) Ltd, Croydon, CR0 4YY.

John Murray Learning policy is to use papers that are natural, renewable and recyclable products and made from wood grown in sustainable forests. The logging and manufacturing processes are expected to conform to the environmental regulations of the country of origin.

John Murray Learning
Carmelite House
50 Victoria Embankment
London EC4Y 0DZ

www.hodder.co.uk

• • • • • •

# ABOUT THE AUTHOR

**Tricia Woolfrey** is an integrative executive coach, business coach and therapist with a background in human resources, training and coaching, hypnotherapy and nutrition.

As an expert in the psychology and physiology of behaviour, performance and productivity, Tricia has a passion for helping people live a successful, fulfilled and balanced life. A proponent of mindfulness and heart-centred living, she works with corporates and private individuals wanting to get the most from their business, career and personal life.

She has a business consultancy and a hypnotherapy/nutritional practice in Harley Street, London, and in Surrey. She works with groups and on a 1:1 basis. She also runs numerous workshops for stress management, presentation skills, influencing skills, time management, personal development, anger management, performance, productivity and wellness.

She has numerous other books, CDs and MP3s to her name. For more information, visit:

www.pw-consulting.co.uk
www.yourempoweredself.co.uk
www.self-help-resources.co.uk
www.triciawoolfrey.com

• • • • • •

# CONTENTS

# INTRODUCTION

Most of us feel tired at one time or another. This can be a natural consequence of an occasional sleepless night, a little overindulgence or working long hours to meet a deadline.

However, if fatigue is a general characteristic of your everyday life it means that there is something out of balance that needs your attention. Ignoring it does not make it go away. Pretending it isn't there doesn't miraculously create an abundance of energy to support you through your day. It certainly doesn't help you deal with life's challenges. A chronic lack of energy can eat away at you until you become a shadow of yourself, sleepwalking through life and becoming a passive passenger, reacting to situations rather than creating the circumstances that are right for you.

Good energy can be yours for the taking if you follow the simple strategies in this book. They will help you deal with all of life's challenges more easily and, better still, will help you enjoy the good times more fully. What's not to love?

Unfortunately, having a good level of energy can seem like an impossible dream to some. As a holistic coach and therapist, I notice that at least 80 per cent of my clients say they would like to have more energy. A good proportion of those describe themselves as feeling as if they are wading through treacle with brain fog a constant companion. That's a lot of people spending a lot of time not at their best.

Energy is a key resource that enables you to get the very most from your day. It even allows you to enjoy your peaceful moments better – a calm energy, if you will. When you take your foot off the pedal, do you sink into an exhausted heap, falling asleep and waking to start the onslaught of life again, feeling drained and unrested? Energy helps you enjoy your peaceful moments in a cocoon of calm tranquillity and emerge feeling rested and motivated.

Wikipedia defines energy as 'the strength and vitality required for sustained physical and mental activity' and 'a feeling of possessing such strength and vitality'.

······

# GOOD ENERGY CAN BE YOURS FOR THE TAKING IF YOU FOLLOW THE SIMPLE STRATEGIES IN THIS BOOK.

······

As I was writing this book, my good friend Linda was listening to Chris Evans interviewing Kenneth Branagh on his breakfast show. In discussing the energy he has on stage, Kenneth quoted William Blake who defined energy as 'eternal delight'. Linda misheard it as 'internal delight', which, I have to admit, I prefer. What a beautiful way to describe it. And, when you think about it, when you are energized, you do feel a sense of positivity that is not forced inwards but instead radiates from within. Whether momentary or eternal, the energy comes from inside you.

Also called Chi or Prana, energy is the life force that circulates throughout your body via the meridians. These are invisible energy channels that serve to transport energy throughout your body and affect every organ and physiological system you have. Acupuncture and acupressure stimulate these points, which is why they can have a calming or energizing effect, depending on what your needs are.

Energy is at the centre of the twin qualities of motivation and drive, and is the characteristic that enables you to get what you want from your day with enthusiasm. Without it, it is impossible to function at your best in all the roles you hold: parent, spouse, partner, son/daughter, brother/sister, employee, business owner, committee member, team worker and any other role you may have.

If you aren't functioning at your best – firing on all cylinders – then you can't undertake your responsibilities to the best of your ability. This can affect your career or your business because it is almost impossible to be fully productive without this vital resource. It can certainly affect your relationships because it is much harder to give of yourself if your energy is low.

- Without energy, you will lack the ability to work or study as well as you can or enjoy your leisure time.

- Without energy, you might find that you are more irritable, less productive and more prone to illness.

- Without energy, problems are more difficult to solve – not only is your energy low but so is your cognitive function – your ability to think clearly.

- Without energy, ideas and creativity are impaired and living a fulfilling life can feel impossible because everything is more difficult than it needs to be.

- Without energy, your emotional resilience – your ability to bounce back from setbacks – is compromised. This means that the little things will affect you as if they are the big things and you will find it difficult to cope.

## Adrenal energy versus core energy

Many people have a high level of nervous energy – you can sense it when you are in their presence. They have a restless 'adrenal' energy and find it hard to switch off. They might show the following signs:

- Foot-tappers can't keep their feet still, even when seated.

- Pacers can't stand still for long, so can often be seen pacing up and down when on their mobiles.

- The hyperactive take multitasking to new levels, doing lots of things very quickly and taking on new projects even though they have an already full load. They pack so much into their day that there is no time just to be.

- Adrenaline junkies and risk takers seek thrills such as high-risk sports like skydiving, or they thrive on drama and leaving things until the last minute.

- Insomniacs have busy brains that keep them awake at night and so they don't get the rest and recuperation they need.

But often, when they stop, these restless people *really* stop – as if the tank has emptied completely. They become submerged into the sofa like an ice cream in its cone on a hot summer's day, seemingly irretrievable to all but the deepest sleep.

A reliance on adrenal energy can lead to adrenal exhaustion, or adrenal fatigue. This happens when your adrenal glands have become over-stimulated and don't function adequately in response to stress. You know you are at risk of this when you need stimulants like sugary food and drinks (including diet versions), coffee or cigarettes (the chemicals they contain include stimulants). There is more on this complex subject in Chapter 8 on exercise and nutrition.

The difference between adrenal energy and core energy is sustainable healthy living.

# Quiz

To understand your energy better, take this quiz. Which of these applies to you? (Mark off as many as you like.)

1. ☐ I wake up tired.
2. ☐ I perk up once I have my first coffee (or three).
3. ☐ I have a lot of energy but, when I stop, I feel as if I'm in a coma.
4. ☐ I feel better as soon as I've eaten something.
5. ☐ My energy perks up when I do something I like.
6. ☐ My energy perks up when I have a deadline looming.
7. ☐ I feel generally rundown and overwhelmed.
8. ☐ I have a calm, stable energy level throughout the day.

Number 8 is the one to aim for. If you said yes to any of the preceding questions, you have come to the right place: this book will help you achieve the utopia that is number 8.

## Physical causes of tiredness

Being tired all the time has many possible culprits, most of which are dealt with in this book. It is important first, however, to rule out any possible physical causes of your lack of energy, which a doctor or health professional would need to address. Here are the main ones:

**THYROID IMBALANCE**
The thyroid gland is responsible for the speed of metabolism and it affects body temperature, circulation, appetite, energy levels and more. The symptoms of poor thyroid function can be similar to CFS and ME (see below), so it's important to ask your doctor to conduct a thyroid test to determine whether this is the cause of your fatigue so that the appropriate treatment can be given.

**CFS – CHRONIC FATIGUE SYNDROME**
This is a blend of tiredness and pain, with extreme tiredness being the main concern. Even brushing your teeth can seem like being asked to swim the Channel with weights attached to your limbs. Often confused with ME, the symptoms are similar. It is not improved by rest and often follows a viral infection. I have found that working on both emotional and physical factors for CFS gives the best results.

**ME – MYALGIC ENCEPHALOPATHY (MYALGIC ENCEPHALOMYELITIS)**
This is a blend of extreme physical and mental tiredness as well as physical pain where they are of equal concern, unlike CFS where fatigue is the main problem. Sufferers will often experience forgetfulness, confusion and difficulty

7

concentrating. It is much misunderstood and (in my humble opinion and experience) has a strong correlation to type A personalities – highly driven, ambitious and perfectionist – who have reached burnout. Rest helps but does not cure. As with CFS, I have found that working on both emotional and physical factors gives the best results.

### LYME'S DISEASE

This disease, though still quite rare, is becoming more common. It is caused by bacteria from a tick bite entering the blood-stream. Symptoms include extreme fatigue, skin rash, fever, headaches and pain. Help should be sought as soon as possible as Lyme's disease can become chronic and, in severe cases, fatal.

### POOR LIVER FUNCTION

Your liver has many functions and is responsible for detoxi-fication. If your liver function is compromised, and you regu-larly wake up between the times of 1 a.m. and 3 a.m. when the liver is most active, it can significantly affect your energy levels and you will wake up feeling tired. Liver function is greatly supported by having good nutrition, so do make sure you read Chapter 8 on exercise and nutrition.

### BLOOD SUGAR IMBALANCE AND TYPE II DIABETES

A stable blood sugar level is essential for good energy, and fatigue will be the consequence of an imbalance. Chapter 8 gives advice on how to balance your blood sugar levels and decrease the chance of acquiring type II diabetes.

**ANAEMIA**

Anaemia is caused by a decrease in the body's ability to carry oxygen around the body and it is important to see your doctor if you suspect this.

**CANDIDIASES**

This is an overgrowth of *Candida albicans*, a naturally occurring yeast that lives in the gut. As well as causing fatigue, it has many other symptoms including headaches, abdominal pain, weight gain and depression.

**AMALGAM FILLINGS**

If you have amalgam fillings you will be absorbing mercury, which is thought to cause fatigue in 86 per cent of patients, according to a study by Bio-Probe, reported in *What Doctors Don't Tell You* in February 2013. You may think that having them removed would be the obvious answer but that could actually make things worse unless a strict protocol is followed to avoid breathing in the fumes created by drilling. Make sure you see a dentist with experience of how to do it properly.

# Psychological causes of tiredness

Tiredness can also be the result of emotional difficulties, so it is important to identify and address these issues. When you don't deal with emotions at their cause, it can lead to depression, so it's essential to take appropriate action early on so that the Big D doesn't take hold. Of course, fatigue is one of the symptoms of depression, too.

## NEGATIVE EMOTIONS

Negative emotions can be tiring. Putting a lid on them, as many of us do, can make them even worse because the effort to suppress and repress them really takes it out of you. If you find you are on an emotional roller coaster or that negative emotions are a key factor in your life, it's really important to get help from someone who not only understands but can also show you how to express and manage them in a healthy way. For more on this subject, see Chapter 6 on inner talk.

## GAD – GENERALIZED ANXIETY DISORDER

Anxiety can also be a great source of fatigue, especially when it is pervasive, long-standing and difficult to control, as in the case of GAD. If you are waking up each morning with a sense of doom and irrational fear filters through all your experiences throughout the day, that anxiety will consume all your energy. Hypnotherapy, mindfulness and the emotional freedom technique (see Appendix I) are all useful ways of dealing with this troubling condition.

## DEPRESSION

Fatigue can be a symptom of depression. If you have had, for at least two weeks, a low mood or loss of pleasure and interest in things you would normally enjoy – together with any of the following: loss of energy, disturbance of appetite (eating more than usual or less than usual), difficulty sleeping, poor concentration, feelings of worthlessness, guilt or hopelessness, withdrawing from relationships – these are signs that you may be depressed and it is helpful to see a professional as soon as possible.

How to use this book

This book is designed to help you to maximize your energy so that you feel that strength and vitality emotionally and physically in all areas of your life. The key words are organized as an acronym, ENERGIZER, which will take you through the different facets of optimizing your energy so that you can enjoy work, rest and play. Here is an overview of the acronym:

**ENVIRONMENT** – how your surroundings energize or deplete you

**NO** – how one little word can free up a lot of energy

**EMPOWERMENT** – how setbacks can energize you and help you evolve

**RESTORERS** – understanding and managing your energy friends and foes

**GOALS** – the importance of focus for sustainable energy

**INNER TALK** – what you say to yourself can be a boost or a blow to your energy

**ZEN** – mindfulness as a calming energy

**EXERCISE AND NUTRITION** – the building blocks of good energy

**REST AND RELAXATION** – the importance of downtime to create more uptime

This book is perfect for you if you feel tired all the time and need more energy to get through the day – either in your personal life or your career. Because reams of reading can, in itself, deplete energy, you might want to take a chapter a week to give you enough time to implement what you learn from each chapter and to ensure that you build on these new skills and habits, absorbing them into your life with a sense of momentum and ease. I will purposely keep to the point so that you get what you need in a way that is simple to absorb and apply.

# Time to reflect

Before you begin, take this quiz to see just how your energy is affecting you now and how prepared you are to make changes:

1. How would you rate your personal energy out of 10, with 10 being fully and appropriately energized?

2. Is low energy affecting your motivation?
   Y / N

3. Is low energy affecting your relationships?
   Y / N

4. Is low energy affecting your work?
   Y / N

5. Is low energy affecting your career\business?
   Y / N

6. Is low energy affecting your leisure and down time?
   Y / N

7. Is low energy affecting your health?
   Y / N

8. Out of 10, how ready are you to make changes so that you can enjoy greater strength and vitality in all areas of your life?

# The hidden benefits of lack of energy

If question 8 in the quiz above yielded a score of less than 7, even though lack of energy feels like a real problem to you, it is likely that you gain some hidden benefit from it that you are not consciously aware of. This is an extremely complex area but below are some of the factors which could be blocking you from making changes:

- **Fear of failure** – if you don't try, you can't be blamed for getting it wrong. True, but if you don't try, you will never improve. Fear of failure is a huge block for many people, often accompanied by a strong perfectionist trait.

- **Fear of success** – sometimes, it is success that is the problem. How easy would it be to maintain? How will people respond to you if you are different? Will they expect even more from you? These are some of the questions that need to be addressed before you are ready to reclaim your energy.

- **Skills** – if you don't know how to achieve more energy, it would not be surprising if you felt unmotivated to work towards it, and this book is designed to help you.

These secondary gains can be difficult to deal with on your own, but become much easier with hypnotherapy, which addresses the problem at an unconscious level – right at its root. The results can be quite enlightening! In the meantime, work through the book diligently and you may find that the secondary gains melt away of their own accord.

This book is designed to provide insights and strategies to facilitate sustainable living and avoid burnout, eliminate brain fog and bring vitality to your life. Are you ready?

Get yourself a highlighter pen (or use the digital highlighter if you are reading this on a tablet) and, as you work through the book, highlight the points that you think will have the biggest impact on you. This has the effect of imprinting it more firmly in the mind. It also helps you to scan the book after you have finished for your best bits, saving you time. Saving time saves energy!

# 1

# ENERGY AND YOUR ENVIRONMENT

......

**How your surroundings energize or deplete you**

•  •  •  •  •  •

Your environment is everything around you – where you live, where you work and where you choose to spend your leisure time. The quality of your environment can have an impact on your energy and your productivity.

Your environment is affected by a number of factors, including clutter, the people you spend your time with, the noise around you (environmental and music), the media (including newspapers, magazines, radio and TV) and the electromagnetic fields that surround you. These can all have an impact on your energy, either positively or negatively. Let's take them one at a time.

## Clutter

It is said that to hoard clutter is to hold on to emotional problems. It is a sign that you are not letting go. In holding on to clutter you are not making space for the new. Too much clutter does not allow energy to flow. When this happens, your personal energy can be blocked, too.

Also, according to the principles of feng shui, it can even affect your health, your relationships, your prosperity, your creativity, your reputation, potential for self-improvement and more. If you feel blocked in one of these areas of your life, it is likely that there is a blockage in the area that represents it. I write more about this in my book *21 Ways and 21 Days to the Life You Want*. For now, let's concentrate on your own personal energy.

Clutter creates stagnancy. This is anathema to energy because it creates lethargy and even depression. Do you know that feeling when you are on the sofa on a Sunday afternoon and it feels like too much effort to get up? Yet if you had been up and about doing something, it would be easy for you to attend to what is required because a moving object has more energy than a stagnant one. As one of Newton's laws states, 'Every object in a state of uniform motion tends to remain in that state of motion unless an external force is applied to it.'

Stagnant energy is difficult to mobilize, so decluttering is key to creating positive flow and energy in your life. One of the first things I do when I am suffering from a big energy dip, especially when it is accompanied by brain fog, is to check my desk and office for clutter. Nine times out of ten, having a quick tidy-up makes all the difference I need to get my energy back on track. What difference do you think it could make for you?

How to declutter, step by step

Here are some tips to help you declutter your environment:

Throw out any old books or magazines.

Get rid of any unfinished projects that you know you will not finish – or delegate (or donate) them to someone who will.

Dispose of any out-of-date paperwork such as old paid bills.

Tidy up any disorder – remember that a clear desk promotes clear thinking and clear thinking is more energy-efficient.

Keep your environment clear of dust and grime.

Rid yourself of anything that is not beautiful, useful or has sentimental value.

When you do this, you will feel much lighter and freer.

You don't have to go crazy about it. The aim is to be free from clutter, not to be starchy or sterile. You may want to consider hiring the services of a feng shui consultant who can give you specific advice related to you and your environment. In the meantime, you may want to invest in some plants. Not only are they beautiful but they also stimulate positive energy and increase oxygen levels.

......

'THE QUALITY OF YOUR ENVIRONMENT CAN HAVE AN IMPACT ON YOUR ENERGY AND YOUR PRODUCTIVITY.'

......

## People

Have you ever noticed that you can spend time with some people and feel completely energized by their presence? These people will tend to be positive, with a relaxed attitude to life. They are unlikely to take themselves too seriously so you don't have to tiptoe around them and you are likely to find that conversation flows easily.

Then there are those who seem to drain you. I like to call these people 'energy parasites'. It is as though they take all their energy from you, just by being in your presence. They may even drain the energy from a room filled with other people. They will typically be negative, cynical and complaining. They may justify this by saying that they are just being realistic, or they are just trying 'to keep it real', or even that you are being naive. But you can certainly be realistic without being a drain on other people.

You can't always choose who you spend time with but you can certainly limit the amount of time you spend with people who deplete your energy and choose to spend more time with those who inspire you and energize you. It is said that we become like the top five people we spend time with, so do choose wisely.

And, while you're at it, ask yourself what kind of energy you bring to others. Do you bring a relaxed energy to those you engage with or do you find people avoiding you or putting up with you reluctantly? Is this something you want to change?

Dr Travis Bradberry published an article on LinkedIn where he describes toxic people:

- **The Gossip** enjoys other people's misfortunes.

- **The Temperamental** is unable to control their emotions.

- **The Victim** doesn't accept responsibility for their situation.

- **The Self-absorbed** uses you as just a tool to help them feel good.

- **The Envious** doesn't enjoy your accomplishments and may belittle them.

- **The Manipulator** is always on the make and has no interest in your needs.

- **The Dementor** is highly negative and has a dark energy.

- **The Twisted** gets pleasure from hurting people.

- **The Judgemental** passes judgement on anything not in alignment with what they consider right and wrong.

- **The Arrogant** hides under a façade of extreme confidence; they feel good when they put people down.

But what can you do about it?

The first thing is to recognize these traits for what they are – a drain on your energy and a blight on your day. The second is to set boundaries and be clear about those boundaries. This is more complicated because a lot depends on your relationship with the toxic person. If you don't have to maintain a relationship with them, you can just make sure they are not a part of your life.

If they have to remain close to you (through work or because they are a family member), it's important to be clear about what you will and will not accept. It is easy to keep prioritizing other people's needs over your own, or deciding that something doesn't really matter. Chapter 2 on how to say no will really help with this one. You may also find this modification of the Serenity Prayer helpful.

••••••

## 'GRANT ME THE SERENITY TO ACCEPT THE PEOPLE I CANNOT CHANGE, THE COURAGE TO CHANGE THE ONES I CAN AND THE WISDOM TO KNOW THAT IT'S ME.'

••••••

## Noise

What is noise to one person is music to another. I have a friend who loves to play loud music when he's concentrating. He finds the music energizing and it helps his creative process. I can't think straight when music is playing and the effort it takes me to think through the noise is tiring. There's no right or wrong in this; it's a personal choice.

If you need an energy boost, what music do you find energizing? What music do you find uplifting? What music do you find brings you down? Creating your own energy playlist can be a simple way of getting a quick shift in your mood and your energy but it's very personal, so it's worth spending an afternoon creating one that's just right for you.

Noise can also relate to environmental noise. If you live under a flight path, for example, or near roadworks, the resulting noise can really affect you – if you let it. When I got married our first home was right underneath a flight path. Every three minutes a plane would fly so low that we could almost wave to the pilot. The noise was deafening but, somehow, we were able to 'zone out' so that it didn't affect us any more. We now live in a quiet area and, when a plane flies over, we look up in surprise. It's all about your perspective and what you focus on.

If you look at the image opposite, you may see either a profile of Salvador Dali or the figure of a woman. If you are finding it difficult to see both, Salvador's eye is the woman's head. You see what you focus on. One might be truer for you, but you know another truth is possible.

I am reminded of those times when I am on a train and someone has their headphones on. If I focus on hearing the percussion of the music with none of the melody, I find the relentless *tsch tsch tsch* incredibly frustrating. Alternatively, if I decide to read my book or do meditation, I will not hear the sound at all. It is all in how I choose to focus.

The image opposite shows how our focus can create our reality. If we focus on noise, that's what we get, along with the energy drop it produces. So, you have a couple of choices:

• Learn to focus on something else.

• Put your headphones in, with music conducive to what you want to achieve.

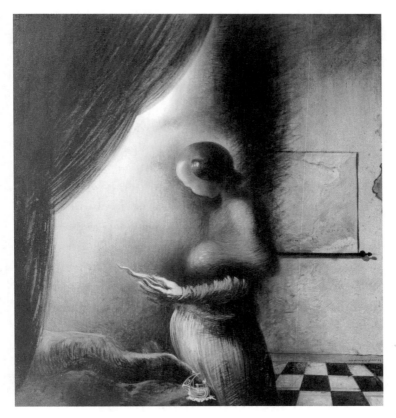

*The Image Disappears No. 1*, 1938 © Salvador Dalí, Fundació
Gala-Salvador Dalí, DACS 2016

# Media exposure

Just as the people we spend time with affect our energy, so do the media we expose ourselves to: newspapers, magazines, radio and TV.

It is useful to think about the effect something has on you when deciding whether it is an energizer or not. For example, when you read the newspaper, do you feel energized by it or depressed? Anything that brings you down brings down your energy level, too. It can't not.

Of course, it is helpful to keep up with what is going on with the world, but it isn't necessary to absorb yourself completely in the negativity of it. Newspapers and news programmes focus primarily on the negative and, in that, they rarely give a balanced view. It's pretty easy to feel wound up afterwards. So make sure you balance your need to keep up to date with positive reading and positive TV and radio. Perhaps limit yourself to headlines unless a subject is really important to you.

# Electromagnetic fields

The jury is still out, but some people believe that electromagnetic fields can produce numerous negative effects such as fatigue, headaches, anxiety, depression and illness – even dementia and tumours. Several organizations refute these claims, but if your energy is low and you don't know why, try removing any electrical items from your bedroom in particular. This includes laptops, TVs, mobiles, base stations and even electrical alarm clocks.

Apart from anything else, the World Health Organization said in 2001 that there might be a link with cancer. While they also said that there was insufficient data to draw conclusions, why take the risk if there are other options? Get yourself an old-fashioned clock, remove everything else electrical from your bedroom except your bedside light and see what difference it makes to you.

In any event, it is not good for your rest to have your laptop, a TV or your mobile in the bedroom as these are too stimulating to the brain, thereby having a detrimental effect on your sleep, leaving you feeling tired in the mornings. Bedrooms are meant for rest, sleep and sex. Full stop.

As a final word on environment, in his book *Truth vs Falsehood*, David Hawkins, who spent 20 years researching levels of human consciousness, describes the findings of Hans Selye (1907–82) – a pioneering scientist who conducted research on our response to stressors. Selye explained stress-reaction patterns as follows: when we have the initial alarm reaction to a stressor, we move into a state of resistance, which in turn causes exhaustion and physiological impairment. This will not only lower our energy levels but also affect whether we have negative or positive energy. Hawkins explains that any stressor with a calibration over 200 creates peace, positive emotions and improves the immune system, whereas anything below 200 creates stress and disease. Here I share with you a few examples given in the book.

| Trait | Stressor calibration |
|---|---|
| Blaming | 180 |
| Critical | 120 |
| Victim/perpetrator | 130–50 |
| Dependable | 250 |
| Diplomatic | 240 |
| Flexible | 245 |
| Humble | 270 |
| Rational | 405 |
| Respectful | 305 |
| Sense of humour | 345 |
| **Movie** | |
| A Beautiful Mind | 375 |
| Bonnie and Clyde | 105 |
| Dickens's Christmas Carol | 499 |
| The Exorcist | 140 |
| Toy Story | 400 |
| **Music** | |
| The Beach Boys | 400 |
| Gangster rap | 35-95 |

| | |
|---|---|
| Andrea Bocelli | 550 |
| Christmas carols | 550 |
| Strauss | 475 |
| **Places** | |
| Airports | 205 |
| *(I thought this would be much lower!)* | |
| Parks | 350 |
| Coffee shops | 250 |
| The Louvre, Paris | 500 |

This demonstrates that the behaviours and activities we engage in will have an impact on the *quality* of our energy – whether our energy is dark and agitated or calm and positive. It's surprising the effect it can have, don't you think?

# Time to reflect

1. Is your home cluttered?

2. Are your cupboards at home cluttered? *(These count too!)*

3. Is your workplace cluttered?

4. Do you keep your environment clean?

5. Do you hoard things like old books, magazines and paperwork?

6. Do you have plants, to stimulate positive energy?

7. Do you have people in your life that leave you feeling drained?

8. Can you reduce the amount of time you spend with them?

9. Can you minimize the effect of these people by making sure that there are positive people around?

10. Do you feel negative after watching the news or reading the papers?

11. Do your TV choices leave you feeling negative, lethargic or uninspired?

12. Can you reduce the electromagnetic fields around you, especially in your bedroom?

If you answered yes to any of the above, which are the top three changes you can make which will have the biggest impact on you?

# 2

# THE VALUE OF SAYING NO

......

**How one little word can free up a lot of energy**

• • • • • •

In this chapter we are going to talk about assertiveness and your ability to set clear boundaries – your ability to say no. What has this got to do with your energy? Well, it could be plenty. Answer the following questions. Do you:

- find yourself saying yes to things you would have preferred to say no to?

- find that you take on more than you can cope with?

- find you are so eager to please that you say yes when, in your heart of hearts, you know you shouldn't?

- say yes to avoid an argument?

- say yes because you fear the consequences of saying no?

- run yourself ragged while those around you aren't pulling their weight?

- take responsibility for other people's happiness or security?

If you answered yes to any of these, it's a sign that you might need to set clearer boundaries with people or assert yourself. Many of us are brought up to believe that being helpful is a good trait and that saying no is selfish. But it's important to remember the basic principle of in-flight safety: always to put your own oxygen mask on before helping others in an emergency. Most parents would agree that this is completely counterintuitive; it's a basic instinct to protect our children. But, to do so, it is important to stay safe ourselves. It is the same with boundaries. By being more respectful of your own needs, you have more to give others. You will also have more self-respect, more self-esteem and more respect from other people – and more energy.

We teach people how to treat us. If you are someone who always says yes, you will always be the first in line when someone needs a favour. To teach people to respect your boundaries, you have to teach them what your boundaries are. I often give a simple assignment to clients suffering from blurred boundaries: to say no to three things during the week. They can be really small, such as 'No, I don't want a second helping', or 'No, I am just finishing something off' or 'No, I don't want a coffee, thanks'. Make it something achievable and you are more likely to do it. This simple exercise has three benefits:

**1.** It starts to build the assertiveness muscle.
**2.** It gets people used to you not being a pushover.
**3.** It strengthens your self-esteem.

# Building self-esteem

Why do we find it so difficult to say no? There can be many reasons, from our upbringing to our beliefs about what it means to be a good person, or fears about the consequences, real or imagined. One of the most common reasons is the fear that people will think badly of us.

I heard a quote once that some people will love you no matter what you do, some people will hate you no matter what you do, but everyone else will like you just fine the way you are. The trouble is that we spend so much time trying to make the wrong people like us and approve of us.

Is there a vegetable you just don't like? A friend of mine really hates cucumbers. Loathes them. Just the mention of them will cause her to wrinkle her nose and curl her lips in disgust. But there is nothing intrinsically wrong with cucumbers. They're just not for her.

It's the same with people. If a few people take a dislike to you, it isn't because there is anything wrong with you. It is just that the chemistry isn't right. There is nothing for you to prove. Their approval of you or otherwise is no measure of your worth. It does not define you. Self-esteem is something that comes from inside you, not outside. Getting people to like you is a most unrewarding sport, and it is corrosive. Spending all your time trying to get those few people to like you is a waste of your energy and it is very liberating to get let go of that need.

••••••

# 'SOME PEOPLE WILL LOVE YOU NO MATTER WHAT YOU DO, SOME PEOPLE WILL HATE YOU NO MATTER WHAT YOU DO, BUT EVERYONE ELSE WILL LIKE YOU JUST FINE THE WAY YOU ARE.'

••••••

In his book *I'm OK – You're OK,* Dr Thomas A. Harris developed the concept of being OK, based on the principles of Transactional Analysis. It's a really useful way of understanding your view of yourself:

You are OK with me

| | I'm not OK<br>You are OK<br>(aka Helpless) | I am OK<br>You are OK<br>(aka Happy) | |
|---|---|---|---|
| I am not OK with me | I am not OK<br>You are not OK<br>(aka Hopeless) | I am OK<br>You are not OK<br>(aka Horrid) | I am OK with me |

You are not OK with me

Building self-esteem is key and, while it is not the focus of this book, here are some tips to help you because self-esteem is energizing.

## EXPAND YOUR COMFORT ZONE

Living within your comfort zone keeps you comfy but makes you fearful of anything outside it. It is impossible to increase your self-esteem when you are fearful, so make sure you are moving outside it on a regular basis so that it expands. As your comfort zone gets bigger, your confidence will expand, too.

## STOP COMPARING YOURSELF

Do you find yourself comparing your 'outtakes' with other peoples' 'edited highlights'? That's a recipe for being negative about yourself. And when you put yourself down, your energy is likely to be down too. It can certainly lead to you having difficulty saying no because it can create a desire to please.

······

'PERSONALITY BEGINS WHERE COMPARISON LEAVES OFF. BE UNIQUE. BE MEMORABLE. BE CONFIDENT. BE PROUD.'

······

*Shannon L. Adler, author*

We don't know what challenges and burdens other people face or what sacrifices they have made to achieve what they have. That's the problem with only seeing people through edited highlights. It is not a true representation of them, only their best self. And you have your best self too. It's time to nurture it.

**LEARN TO LIKE YOURSELF**

If you've been playing the comparison game, doubtless you don't feel too good about yourself. Yet you have friends who choose to spend time with you. You have family who love you, despite your faults. So my invitation to you is to write a list of the things you *do* like about yourself. Many people find this really difficult. If necessary, think of what your friends, loved ones and colleagues would say. If you are still struggling, ask them. But get yourself a list. Write it down on a nice piece of card and look at it often. These qualities are the truth about who you are. Focusing on what you do like about you rather than what you don't like about you can prompt a huge shift in your self-esteem and help increase your self-belief, which lets you say no when you need to.

Here is a list of traits borrowed from my book *21 Ways and 21 Days to the Life You Want*, which might help you in forming your own list:

| | | | |
|---|---|---|---|
| Considerate | Determined | Easy-going | Funny |
| Friendly | Generous | Good listener | Honest |
| Intelligent | Kind | Loving | Loyal |
| Open | Organized | Passionate | Positive |
| Practical | Reliable | Sense of humour | |

**OVERCOME LIMITING BELIEFS**

Beliefs are those thoughts that you treat as if they are true, for example 'I'm not good enough', 'Good people always say yes' or 'Saying no is selfish'. We act as though they are true but there is no truth in them. They are just thoughts. Limiting beliefs are the ones that stand in the way of your feeling good about yourself, your happiness and your success. Empowering beliefs are those that are supportive of you. An easy way to deal with limiting beliefs is to create empowering ones that act as an antidote to them. For example:

| Limiting belief | Empowering belief |
|---|---|
| I'm not good enough. | I'm a good and worthwhile person. |
| Good people always say yes. | Good people know when to say yes and when to say no with grace. |
| Saying no is selfish. | Saying no kindly is the sign of a confident and discerning person. |
| Other peoples' needs are more important than mine. | My needs are valid. |

Empowering beliefs need to be repeated many times to counteract the negative beliefs, so do persist – it's worth the

41

effort. There is a more robust method described in my book *21 Ways and 21 Days to the Life you Want*.

What are your limiting beliefs? What empowering beliefs can you identify which would neutralize them?

## FOCUS ON YOUR ACHIEVEMENTS

You have got to where you are through effort, whether or not you think you should have tried harder or achieved more. Don't believe me? As a baby you couldn't walk or talk. Learning these skills is highly complex and you did it. You didn't give up walking the first time you fell down. You just kept trying until you were able to walk without thinking. The same went for learning to talk. There are many more achievements you have made along the way – surviving your first day at school, winning that swimming certificate, passing exams, learning to drive, getting your first job, and earning that promotion you wanted. No matter how big or small, your life is strewn with achievements. Somehow, as we grow up, we learn to ignore those and focus on what we haven't yet achieved. This leaves us feeling 'less than' and can lead to feelings of inferiority and a need to get approval.

Make a list of all your achievements, big and small, and perhaps put it on the reverse side of the card with the traits you like about yourself. Look at it often as a reminder of your ability to learn and grow.

## ACCEPT IMPERFECTION

Perfection is not a human condition, yet so many people beat themselves up for not being absolutely perfect at anything or, worse, everything. Perfection, as they say, is a journey, not a destination. It is more useful to see your life as progress, not use perfection as a tyrannical master. Beating yourself up for not being perfect erodes your self-esteem just as rain dissolves snow.

# Fear of not being needed

We all like to feel needed – it is one of the ways we achieve meaning in our lives, a sense of purpose and a sense of worth. For some, this need can result in martyrdom – a way of feeling important and alive by exaggerating our suffering or playing the victim in order to gain sympathy and support or to feel superior.

It makes those around you at best beholden and at worst lazy or irresponsible. But, as Dr Henry Cloud and Dr John Townsend say in their book *Boundaries*, you can't terrorize or make others feel guilty and be loved by them at the same time. So the question is, do you prefer to be needed or loved? As a strategy for securing love, making yourself indispensable is flawed. It can even create resentment.

If you are creating learned helplessness in those you love because of your desire to be needed, you may be telling yourself that you are being kind and wanting to protect them from harm. But in doing so, you are denying them their entitlement to grow as an individual in their own right. You are affirming their role as victim.

## THE DRAMA TRIANGLE MODEL

Psychotherapist Stephen Karpman created a model of dysfunctional interaction he called the drama triangle, shown here. It looks at how we can get stuck in certain behaviours in ways that are disempowering.

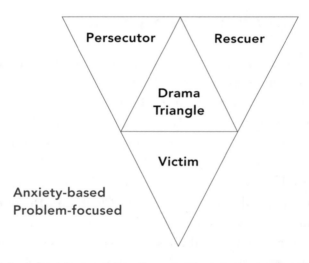

Adapted with permission from Stephen B. Karpman, M.D, author of *A Game of Free Life: The new transactional analysis of intimacy, openness, and happiness* (2014).

**The Victim** tends to be defensive, submissive or passive-aggressive. They rarely accept responsibility for a situation, tend to be very sensitive and often feel powerless to improve their circumstances.

**The Rescuer**, as the name implies, intervenes to rescue the Victim. This may seem like a benevolent position but it actually creates dependence and helplessness in the Victim, effectively keeping them stuck. This may be from a need to be needed, or because it serves the Rescuer well to have the Victim dependent for some reason – for example, to feel stronger, important, to have a sense of purpose or to be seen as heroic/saintly/benevolent.

The Rescuer can also refer to behaviour rather than a person you depend on to feel better. Examples include alcohol, comfort eating, indulging in retail therapy, gambling or smoking as a coping mechanism for life's stressors. If you ever find that you reach for a glass of the strong stuff or your favourite food when you feel low, or any 'too-muching' behaviour, be assured that you are invoking the Rescuer. Again, it may seem like a harmless spot of indulgence, but it keeps you stuck in the drama triangle whether you realize it or not. And this does little for sustainable energy.

**The Persecutor** can be a situation (such as being made redundant or diagnosed with cancer) or a person, such as someone bullying or intimidating you at work. Essentially, the Persecutor is the alleged cause of the Victim's problems as the Victim perceives it, whether intended or not.

What's interesting about the drama triangle is that there

is no virtue in it; there are no real winners, no insights, no growth. The Victim doesn't learn and doesn't change. It is also interesting that the positions are not set in stone. The Rescuer can become the Persecutor if, for example, the Victim does not want to be rescued. 'Stop interfering and let me get on with my life' is a sure sign that the Rescuer has become the Persecutor.

The Persecutor can trade places with the Victim if the Victim takes a stand. You have probably witnessed a bully being confronted and suddenly making excuses, backing down or bursting into tears. I have also seen situations where the Victim can become the Rescuer to the Persecutor if the original Rescuer becomes aggressive on behalf of the Victim. It gets complicated, doesn't it? The point of the drama triangle is that you are stuck in it – your role may change, but you are still in it – unless you do something different. But what?

### UPTURNING THE DRAMA TRIANGLE

In his book *The Power of TED (The Empowerment Dynamic)*, David Emerald talks about turning the drama triangle upside down to create a more empowered perspective, one that is outcome-focused rather than problem-focused.

**The Victim becomes the Creator** of their own life instead of a victim of circumstances. Instead of being a victim of redundancy, they use the opportunity to decide what they want from their future career; instead of asking 'Why me?'

following a cancer diagnosis, they start taking control of their wellbeing and deciding how they can make the most of their lives (this is how my mother dealt with her own diagnosis and how I dealt with my own much less serious one); instead of bowing down to the bully at work, the Creator takes a stand (bullies only bully those in whom they see vulnerability – they will soon leave to find a new target). The Creator becomes focused on what they *do* want rather than focused and submerged in what they *don't* want.

**The Persecutor becomes the Challenger.** Because the Victim becomes the Creator, the Persecutor does not have the same level of power and instead becomes the Challenger to instigate positive action. It's like an invitation to reveal more depths and new skills. We grow best through challenge and adversity, not by everything going smoothly in life. Life is just not like that anyway; so the Creator chooses to allow challenges to better them, not diminish them. It encourages growth when you let challenges be your teacher.

**The Rescuer becomes the Coach.** Instead of rescuing the Victim, the Coach provides encouragement and asks empowering questions to help the Creator move forward – questions such as:

- 'What outcome are you looking for?'
- 'What do you want to do about this?'
- 'What is your next step?'

- 'What is the lesson in this?'
- 'If there were a silver lining here, what would it be?'

Unlike the Rescuer who will lead, the Coach encourages the Creator to take 'response-ability' (to make mindful and empowering choices) and to learn from experience.

The need to be needed is fuel to the drama triangle so, if you find yourself in the triangle more than is healthy, practise the role of Coach. You will release some of your energy to where it will have a more positive effect. Being needed does not mean you have to be the person who takes responsibility for how everybody is. In fact, as this section proves, it can actually be damaging.

# Fear of losing your job

When I worked in the corporate world, I was always struck by the fact that the people who really got on, who were recognized for their contributions both financially and in promotions, were those who knew very well how to say no. If they couldn't meet a deadline, they said so or gave reasons for why they hadn't met it. If they were taking a few days off when there was an important meeting to attend, they simply said they couldn't make it. They did so with such confidence and conviction that they were rarely questioned. They often turned up late and had long lunches. Again, it was not a problem because they assumed it as a right.

Of course, this won't work for everyone; there has to be a base level of respect and trust rather than underperformance. But the observation was that saying no was not career limiting.

Compare that to the conscientious, unassuming worker – the one who is always in early, who works through their lunch break, works late and will cancel a day off in the interests of the business. Yet, inexplicably, they get overlooked. While the great bonus pot is being distributed, it goes to the assertive and the bold. When promotions are being considered, they go to the ones who put themselves forward and ask for what they want.

It isn't fair, but my many years of experience in the corporate world have taught me that this is the reality for many people. That is, unless you are blessed with an observant and fair-minded boss, in which case count yourself very, very lucky.

It's so important to ask for what you want and to say no to what you don't, so that you are taken seriously. People learn to respect you, you respect yourself better and you are not taken for granted. Your self-esteem will increase too. And, of course, so will your energy.

**CHALLENGE YOUR THINKING**

In her book *Loving What Is*, Byron Katie explains what she calls the Work, which challenges your thinking and invites you to explore four perspectives on a situation. This often reveals a greater truth than our initial assumptions.

For example, if you think 'They take me for granted', you might want to withdraw from the effort but you are more likely to redouble your efforts in the hope of attracting the appreciation you deserve – which rarely happens. Katie recommends that you turn around the statements in three different ways:

| | |
|---|---|
| **Original statement:** | '*They* take *me* for granted.' |
| **Turnaround 1:** | '*I* take *them* for granted.' |
| **Turnaround 2:** | '*I* take *me* for granted.' |
| **Turnaround 3:** | 'They *should* take me for granted.' |

Let's take a look at each of these.

**Turnaround 1:** '*I* take *them* for granted.' Could this be true? Yes, it could. Though it is their job, it's hard for a manager to have everybody on their radar, particularly when they are under pressure themselves and under the scrutiny of their own bosses and other stakeholders, especially when a particular someone (you) is so skilled at being unassuming. It is easy to take for granted just how difficult being a manager is and to ignore some of the good things they do, choosing instead to focus on the negative.

Remember that 'They take me for granted' is a Victim comment. You need to move into Creator mode to get out of it. What do you want to create instead?

**Turnaround 2:** '*I* take *me* for granted.' How true is that? This is usually a light-bulb moment with my clients. It is usually the most true statement of them all, but maybe not the most comfortable to acknowledge. A Victim would feel bad about it, and say things like, 'I'm useless', 'I'm pathetic', 'I've ruined everything', 'If only I were a better person, this would never have happened.' You get the drift.

By contrast, the Creator would see this insight as a gift – and completely energizing. Why? Because it means they are in charge of the way people see them and the way they see themselves. Even if you got it wrong before, you don't have to keep getting it wrong. You can change that now. Right now.

How can you do this? By appreciating your own contribution more. By valuing your positive qualities as much as if they belonged to someone else. By being more visible, being a little less modest and owning up to your achievements. If you don't, no one else will. Worse, they might claim your achievements as their own. Are you ready to step up?

Here are some examples of claiming your achievements:

- 'I'm really proud of this project. It took me a long time to work out the elements that blocked our progress but I am pleased to say that the strategy I am proposing not only reduces costs but increases customer satisfaction.' Isn't this better than 'Oh, it's nothing'?

- Or, for a domestic example: 'I'm really proud that I have brought up two children who are respectful of others and kind to each other. I'm not saying it was easy, it wasn't. It is a constant balance between boundaries, freedom and support. But it was worth the effort.' Isn't that better than 'I have nice kids'?

They don't have to be huge achievements for you to own them, either. A simple 'I'm pleased to have got that report in on time' or 'I like the way this new recipe turned out' are enough to validate yourself.

> It's really important to own your achievements, to give yourself credit, and to appreciate your value so that others can too.

**Turnaround 3:** 'They *should* take me for granted.' I always struggled with this one but it makes sense once you get your head around it. 'Really? Why should they?' I would ask myself. I realized that I have an idealistic set of rules that would have everyone being thoughtful for everyone else; world peace follows; everybody is happy. It sounds simple, but it's wholly unrealistic. The Work says that if you are taking yourself for granted, why shouldn't anyone else? You are constantly teaching people how to treat you. It's time to turn the tide and that change starts with you. If you notice that others are taking you for granted, it is time to look to yourself to find out how you are contributing to the problem so that you can make changes. In this lies power, growth, confidence – and energy.

# Crisis addiction

Are you addicted to crises? Do you leave things until the last minute so you have a mini-crisis on your hands from which you can rescue the world? Or do you just like the feeling of adrenaline coursing through your veins? If you are reading this book because your energy is low, crisis addiction may very well be the cause.

There could be various reasons for this. You may need to:

- show your 'superhuman' powers
- indulge your need to be needed
- feel important
- fight fires all the time because you would be bored if you didn't
- feed your 'fix' because you have become an adrenaline junkie.

The danger is that crisis addiction could reach such proportions that you are at risk of burnout. This could ultimately result in your downfall. It's a little like Superman's susceptibility to the effects of kryptonite, which weakens him. For you, crisis addiction – your kryptonite – can eventually weaken you. It can certainly tire you out. And, to add more to the toxic load, it makes you a contributor to other people's stress and energy levels, too.

Superman was only able to renew his superpowers when he got rid of the kryptonite (your crisis addiction). The message here is that you will achieve more by doing less. It can be exhausting being around people who lurch from one crisis to another, so it is no wonder that you yourself are exhausted. It is also important that you start defining yourself differently. It is highly unlikely that your loved ones love you because of this trait, rather *despite* it. You are worth more than that, aren't you?

If you are addicted to the adrenaline rush, it may be that you don't feel alive unless your heart is beating so fast it feels as if it will jump right out of your chest. This may be fun while you are on a high, but when you stop you probably collapse into exhaustion, unable to function. In the long term it is unhealthy. It is really important to have a balance – have your fun but offset it with quiet time, perhaps meditating, or with mindfulness or self-hypnosis (see Chapter 7); then you can enjoy a calmer energy between adventures. Mindfulness allows you to enjoy the moment, to be fully present, rather than hurtling between one thing and another in a frenzy of activity. Self-hypnosis achieves the same thing while reprogramming your mind to be the kind of person you want to be. In this way, excitement can be enjoyed from a foundation of balance. You will be easier to be around too, and that's got to be good, right?

# Fear of being thought selfish

Do you worry that making people responsible for themselves and their choices mean that they will judge you as mean? By denying people their right to make their own mistakes and to do things for themselves, you are denying their right to their own personal development, or you are colluding with their lack of personal responsibility (as I like to call it, response-ability). Neither of these is good for them, or for you.

You can say no *and* be kind. They are not mutually exclusive. It is important for others to learn to appreciate boundaries – including yours. In addition, if you consistently rescue another individual, then you are colluding with their problem, effectively keeping them stuck while deluding yourself that you are being kind or selfless, as though it is a virtue without cost.

Sometimes tough love is the greatest kindness of all – it yields long-term results instead of alleviating short-term wants. If you are constantly saving people from the consequences of their actions, they will find that the same problems come up again and again because you are denying them the opportunity to learn from their experiences. You have yourself trapped in the drama triangle and the only way out is by becoming empowered and by empowering others.

Selfishness is about caring for our own needs without caring about the negative consequences caused to others by our decisions. While we are not responsible *for* others, as long as our decisions don't harm them (see below), it is not selfish. It's self-care.

# Fear of losing love

If you are saying yes to keep the love of another person and it is the only thing that seems to work, then it is not true love. It is an illusion perpetuated by your actions to please. And it is conditional – meaning that if you don't continue to please, love will be withdrawn or withheld. They love your acquiescence. They love the control. I hate to break it to you, but it has nothing to do with true love. True love is *un*conditional – where you are loved for who you are, not who you could be or what you do, how you dress, etc. You are loved despite your faults and perhaps even because of them. It certainly does not rely on you saying yes to something you want to say no to.

If you fear losing love, there is a strong chance that there are issues of self-esteem. This often has a devastating effect on your energy because positive indicators (e.g. 'You look lovely today') boost energy, but negative ones (e.g. 'That outfit looks awful on you') can create the shoulder slump and your energy slumps right along with them. The most important relationship of all is the one you have with yourself. Learn to love yourself – unconditionally – so that you can attract a mutually respectful and loving relationship where you feel secure and deserving based on who you are as a person, not what you do.

Anyone who tells you 'If you loved me, you would...' just wants control over you. True love requires that you allow the other to be themselves. Wanting to change them means they aren't loveable as they are. Of course, this has to be taken in the context of the dance of compromise. But the compromise doesn't all have to come from you. If you are constantly compromising your own needs so that someone else can be happy or to avoid an argument, it is not a healthy relationship. It is worth repeating that you are not responsible for other people's happiness, success, choices or well-being. You are responsible only for yours.

In my work with clients, I see that sometimes they do feel responsible for others, but this is not mirrored by the intent or the actions in those others, who simply go through life relying on others for their happiness and blaming them when things go wrong.

## Fear of hurting someone's feelings

As already mentioned, we teach people how to treat us. I will probably repeat this idea again because it's so important. If we constantly say yes to things, we teach people that we are always there for them, that nothing is ever an issue and that we don't have needs of our own. These won't be conscious thoughts but they will be underlying assumptions made about us, which drive people to turn to us as a first port of call whenever there is a need. This depletes not only our internal resources (our energy) but also our self-respect if we don't start saying no to others and yes to ourselves instead.

Saying yes as a strategy to protect people from being hurt doesn't work if it hurts you. I recently had a client who was run ragged managing a family business and also taking care of all her family's needs and problems, including babysitting for her grandchildren whenever she was asked. No matter what plans she had made for herself, she would cancel them to accommodate others.

She was incredibly exhausted and stressed. I gave her a homework task: she was to say no to at least three requests that week. She almost went white at the thought of this, but agreed to try. Her main concerns were a) How will they cope? and b) Will they be offended/think she has become stroppy? I coached her on how to say no kindly (see below) and off she went.

······

'YOU ARE NOT RESPONSIBLE FOR OTHER PEOPLE'S HAPPINESS, SUCCESS, CHOICES OR WELLBEING. YOU ARE RESPONSIBLE ONLY FOR YOURS.'

······

It was a revelation to her. To her amazement, not only were they unfazed but they were very quick to find someone else to help or to go out another night instead. Her confidence shot up. Her fear of what people would think disappeared and her concern about their ability to cope took a much-needed rest.

Remember that doing things for others indiscriminately is not a sign of the depth of your love – there are much better ways to show that! If you are constantly rescuing loved ones, it is a co-dependent relationship. You can't live the person's life for them, you can't grow for them, you can't make choices for them, you can't learn for them. These are all things they have to do for themselves. It's a case of tough love and you can say no graciously so that their feelings are less hurt, if indeed they are hurt at all.

'THE HARDEST PART OF RAISING A CHILD IS TEACHING THEM TO RIDE BICYCLES. A SHAKY CHILD ON A BICYCLE FOR THE FIRST TIME NEEDS BOTH SUPPORT AND FREEDOM. THE REALIZATION THAT THIS IS WHAT THE CHILD WILL ALWAYS NEED CAN HIT HARD.'

*Sloan Wilson, writer*

I use this quote by Sloan Wilson with many of my clients, whether or not they have children. If you are a natural carer, it is so tempting to save people from themselves, taking the handlebars of the bike and steering them in the right direction, holding the bike upright so that they don't fall over. But, in doing so, the child never learns to ride the bicycle. They are denied that pleasure through your over-caring. They are deprived of the energizing sense of achievement in overcoming a hurdle – one of life's great pleasures. You know that feeling when you achieved something that scared you and you were completely elated? What happened to your energy? And if you had felt hurt by someone not helping you, what happened to that hurt? My guess is that it evaporated, transformed by the excitement. Saying no can be the gift that someone needs. It is much better to belong to the Empowerment Dynamic Club than the Drama Triangle Club, don't you think?

In their book *Boundaries*, Dr Henry Cloud and Dr John Townsend distinguish between hurt and harm. Often, a little hurt actually helps someone. They tell a story of going to the dentist to deal with a cavity. It hurt but it helped them. But the sugar they ate, which caused the cavity in the first place, didn't hurt them but it did harm them. There is a huge difference, so it is worth asking:

- Will this hurt?
- Will this harm?
- Will this help?

Sometimes a hurt can motivate others to step up and take responsibility for themselves.

## How to say no

Saying no is an art form but it's easy to learn. And, if you remember that we teach people how to treat us, your motivation to practise these techniques will hopefully be high.

First of all, let's distinguish between four levels of confidence:

**Passive** – This where you believe the other person has all the rights and you have none.

**Assertive** – This is where you both have equal rights – your thoughts, feelings and needs are as valid as the other person's.

**Aggressive** – This is where it seems that the other person has all the rights and you have none.

**Passive-aggressive** – This is where you don't want to enter into any conflict so you meet your needs under the radar.

| Aggressive | Assertive | Passive | Passive-aggressive |
|---|---|---|---|
| I win, you lose | Win–win | You win, I lose | You think you win, but I do – ha! |
| *Style:* Intimidation | *Style:* Collaboration | *Style:* Capitulation | *Style:* Indirect insubordination |

It is important to remember that your thoughts, feelings and needs are as valid as the other person's. At the same time, you need to accept responsibility for your own perceptions, feelings and actions but *not* the other person's. They are entirely responsible for themselves – whatever they may tell you.

Assertiveness is about appropriately confronting a situation in a respectful, gracious way. It is not about tolerating or accommodating where it is detrimental. It comes from positive self-esteem.

It is a common misperception that aggressive people are extremely confident but that is not true. They hide their low self-esteem behind a veneer of superiority and grandiosity.

But how do you *do* assertiveness? Here is an example. Let's say that your boss has asked you to work late this evening when you have your daughter's school concert to attend / you promised to take your wife out to dinner / you have concert tickets with a friend (delete as appropriate). Here is how it might go:

**YOUR BOSS** We have an important deadline to meet and I need you to work late this evening.

**YOU, KINDLY** I'm sorry but I have other plans this evening, which can't be changed.

**YOUR BOSS** But this is really important.

**YOU, KINDLY** I know this is important to you. I can't work late this evening because I have other plans, which can't be changed.

**YOUR BOSS** But you always help when we need it and this is really important.

**YOU, KINDLY** I can't work late this evening because I have other plans, which can't be changed.

A number of techniques have been used here:

1. **'Acknowledging'** – This is acknowledging where the other person is: 'I know this is important to you.'

2. **'Because'** – The word 'because' has a strong influence when used with the other two techniques. Curiously, this

is true even if there is no connection between the cause and effect!

**3.** '**Stuck record**' – This is where the same point is repeated again and again, rather than engaging in a debate about why. This makes it very difficult to argue. When you over-explain yourself, you weaken your message, as though you are trying to convince yourself of your point of view.

Let's take another example. Suppose a friend asks you, once again, to organize the Christmas party. You do it every year. People offer to help but they rarely do their bit, so you always end up doing more than anyone else and you have decided that you want things to be different this year. You don't mind helping, but you are not happy with doing it all. Here is how it might go:

**YOUR FRIEND** So, what are you planning for the Christmas party this year?

**YOU, KINDLY** I am not planning anything because I am having a year off. I'm looking forward to someone else taking their turn.

**YOUR FRIEND** But you always do such a good job.

**YOU, KINDLY** Thank you, but this year I am taking a year off so someone else can take their turn.

YOUR FRIEND  But no one can do it better than you.

YOU, KINDLY  It's kind of you to say so, but I'm sure someone else can do a good if not better job and I am taking a year off.

YOUR FRIEND  Why are you being so selfish?

YOU, KINDLY  I'm simply allowing someone else to take their turn because I'm taking a year off this time.

Again, the stuck record technique is being used here and it is really hard to argue with. I have actually added some softeners so it isn't so strong, but it is still effective. The word 'because' is being used again, which subtly strengthens the message. The phrase 'this time' softens it and has a subtext: you have done it before and it is perfectly reasonable not to keep doing it. People run out of steam when you use this technique. A reasonable person will see the reasonableness of your stance. An unreasonable person, of course, will still want you to do it. But that's good information, because it shows that they are not considering your needs. This is a signal for you to set firm boundaries – which you are. So all's good.

To make this more collaborative, you could say, 'Since I'm having a year off, who do you think will do the organizing this year?' This puts the problem at their door in a non-confrontational way.

# Words aren't enough

Having said all the above, your words themselves account for only 7 per cent of your communication. Your body language carries a stronger message and accounts for 55 per cent of what you say. Here are some examples of what the different styles might look like:

- **Passive:** hands in pockets, behind back or in the 'fig leaf' position, difficulty making eye contact

- **Aggressive:** arms folded, hands on hips, strong and hard eye contact

- **Assertive:** arms at your side, firm but gentle eye contact

Your tone of voice accounts for an astonishing 38 per cent of your communication, no matter what words you use:

- **Passive:** soft tone with the 'antipodean lift' at the end, as though you are asking a question rather than making a statement

- **Aggressive:** strong and forceful tone

- **Assertive:** a low tone, which creates a stronger credibility in your message, especially when you drop your voice at the end of the sentence

Try saying 'I can't work late this evening because I have other plans, which can't be changed' when not meeting the other person's gaze, with a quiet but high-pitched voice which lifts at the end of the sentence.

Compare that to saying the same sentence with a low but firm tone that drops at the end of the sentence, gently holding the person's gaze with your arms by your side. There's a huge difference, isn't there?

Part of being able to say no is to be credible when you do it.

When you continually say yes to what you want to say no to, it not only takes your energy from a 'doing too much' perspective, but the resentment felt by feeling taken advantage of is also fatiguing. At the same time, the erosion of your self-esteem has a huge effect, too. Just think of the difference you will feel when you start to respect your own needs as though they are as valid as everyone else's – which, of course, they are.

······

# 'PART OF BEING ABLE TO SAY NO IS TO BE CREDIBLE WHEN YOU DO IT.'

······

# Time to reflect

1. Would you classify yourself as passive, assertive, aggressive or passive-aggressive when it comes to dealing with requests for your time and support?

2. What do you need to do to bring your responses into the assertiveness band?

3. Where in your life could saying no more have a positive influence on your energy?

4. What limiting beliefs are standing in your way of creating clear boundaries?

5. What empowering beliefs can you adopt instead? Repeat these ten times every morning in front of the mirror and three times each time you say the negative belief to yourself.

# 3
# EMPOWERMENT AND GROWTH

· · · · · ·

**How setbacks can energize
you and help you evolve**

•   •   •   •   •   •

Do you find yourself feeling despondent and de-energized if something goes wrong or if someone gives you negative feedback? And do you feel energized and happy if you get positive feedback?

Shelle Rose Charvet is an international expert in the field of neuro-linguistic programming and, in her book *Words That Change Minds*, she introduces the concept of meta-programs. They are the way we perceive information and influence our behaviour. One of the metaprograms is the internal/external concept:

- **An internal person** knows within themselves if they have a done a good job. If they don't get feedback, they are OK because they still know how well they've done without it.

- **An external person** has no internal reference and needs outside input to validate them (or not). In the absence of any validation, most of them will assume that they have done a bad job and will often feel very low and demotivated.

The same is true on a personal level. Let's say that Ann is externally referenced. She has just had her hair done and is wearing a new outfit. She feels great. Her husband says nothing. Suddenly her mood changes from good to low in the blink of an eye. She is likely to assume that her husband hates her hair and hates her outfit. It is a challenging meta-program to run with. On the one hand, an externally referenced person will respond to feedback, but they will deflate in the absence of it.

By contrast, an internally referenced person may be closed to feedback – after all, they know just how things are; they don't need you to tell them! The downside, of course, is that they may not accept feedback that is valid. They will be closing the door to growth in a completely different way. But their confidence will be high.

The confidence of an externally referenced person will fluctuate according to the input they are receiving. Their locus of control is outside of them. And it's not a positive position to be in because high confidence is the cousin to high energy. When your confidence drops, so does your energy.

## Growth through challenges

Of course we all love positive feedback; it is nice to have our ego massaged now and again. But something I have noticed over the years, both in myself and in my clients, is that the most important life lessons are not learned from when things go right but when things go wrong. By looking at feedback differently – as a gift of learning and development and growth – it can spur you into motivated action to improve and evolve.

I am reminded of Steve who had a fear of presenting. He was a new business salesperson for a technology company. This meant that he had to present to prospects and win contracts rather than take care of existing customers, which was a different skillset. He was actually fine presenting to new clients. He had a passion for the technology and he liked to help people find the right solution for themselves.

The problem came when he had to present to the board of his own company. They already knew the technology so he was not going to enthral them with that. His issue was that without the 'I'm here to help you' hat on, he had nothing to hide behind. The board wanted to know the numbers. Confident in front of clients, he felt exposed in front of his bosses, none of whom were particularly forthcoming with praise for his performance, despite the results he was getting.

He realized that his confidence was as a consequence of the positive feedback from his prospects and resulting sales he achieved – there is nothing like a signed contract to let you know you did a good job!

His lack of confidence was because he didn't get that feedback from his bosses. The result was that his presentations were flat – he was presenting through a filter of 'Am I doing this right? Do they like what I'm saying?' When you communicate through such self-judgement, it is very difficult to shine. It will almost certainly make your interaction hesitant and self-conscious and is unlikely to inspire confidence in what you have to say.

How could he use this to evolve?

## TAKE 'RESPONSE-ABILITY'

The first step was to acknowledge that he was putting himself in this situation and he could get himself out of it. It is easy to blame others for how you feel but actually we are responsible for our own feelings. It is how we interpret situations, what we choose to absorb and what we choose to simply observe. Response-ability is the power to choose your response to any situation.

## CREATE A RESOURCEFUL STATE

Then, prior to any meeting, he needed to get himself into a resourceful state. By this I mean that, instead of feeling vulnerable and disempowered, he needed to make sure he entered the meeting feeling strong, confident, calm and resourceful – able to respond to the situation appropriately and intuitively. This is easier said than done but, at the same time, it is easier than you think.

If you remember an occasion you were dreading – let's say it was a meeting – doubtless your mental landscape beforehand was everything you were dreading about it. You may have imagined messing up an important point you wanted to make, or the disapproving look of someone you wanted to impress, or perhaps the disinterest of other people as they talked among themselves, ignoring what you had to say. We have a tendency to have a mental rehearsal of how we expect things to go. If you are dreading something, you are setting yourself up for a challenging time, almost inviting the worst to happen. If, on the other hand, you think of a time when you felt really good, confident, in control and able to influence effectively, you are more likely to enter that meeting in a good position to get a positive outcome.

Alternatively, think of something or someone that gives you a warm glow – perhaps your partner, your dog, or a memory of a happy time. When you allow yourself to become absorbed into the positive event (what you see, what you hear and what you feel), it becomes a more constructive filter through which you can experience what you were previously dreading.

If you find that you rely on positive feedback to feel good about yourself, you are setting yourself up for a very difficult life, since most people simply don't think to give you the positive strokes you need. Most people are simply absorbed in their own experience, oblivious to the effect this has on you. This does not mean that they think ill of you. It is important not to jump to negative conclusions in the absence of positive feedback but to evaluate your own performance in any given area.

## CREATE A POSITIVE OUTCOME

The next thing Steve needed to do was to determine the outcome he wanted to achieve. Many people who suffer the negative effects of being externally referenced are also in the habit of thinking of what they *don't* want instead of what they *do* want. This has the effect of focusing you on the negative rather than the positive. Your actions are geared to what you focus on. Focus on the negative and you're likely to get a negative result. Focus on the positive and a good result is more probable because your actions are geared towards what you focus on.

What 'don't want' outcome could Steve have had? Perhaps it was 'to avoid coming across as incompetent or ineffective in front of my bosses'. Can you see how that focuses him on incompetence and ineffectiveness? When you have that mental filter, it tends to taint your interactions in a negative way.

Let's say he chose a positive outcome, such as 'to communicate my achievement of targets and my healthy pipeline confidently'. This is likely to elicit within Steve a much more constructive mindset, not burdened by doubt or fear but bolstered by the very confidence his prospects enjoyed.

······
'WHEN YOUR CONFIDENCE DROPS, SO DOES YOUR ENERGY.'
······

# The 3:1 technique

I like to teach my clients the 3:1 technique. This reinforces self-esteem and the good things you do while allowing you the luxury – and joy – of developing and evolving. Here is how to do it.

In any situation of challenge, think about three things you did well in that and think of one thing you could do differently in hindsight. A lot of people struggle with finding three good things. That's no surprise because those same people are in the habit of finding fault with themselves. They have become blind to success, bypass achievements and ignore results. Instead, they get the metaphorical magnifying glass out and find as much fault as possible, which leaves them feeling incompetent, unworthy and drained.

There is a reason that the ratio is 3:1. By emphasizing the positive, you are reinforcing what is good so that you do more of it. Three positives to one constructive, or negative if you prefer. This has the effect of neutralizing the tendency to be self-critical without ignoring what could be improved. You may have noticed the wording I use for the :1 bit: 'what you would do differently in hindsight'. The wording is purposely positive; there is no implied punishment. It is simply an observation of areas that could be done better next time so that you are constantly learning and growing. Hindsight is a good teacher, so this technique consciously calls upon its wisdom.

Let's take an example to illustrate. Jennifer was anxious about asserting what she wanted to her friends and her boyfriend in particular. While on one level she didn't mind – she liked to make people happy – on the other hand, she never got to do what she wanted. Nobody knew because she never said anything. She adopted the 3:1 technique next time with her boyfriend when she wanted to go to the cinema and he wanted to go the pub. Here is how she asked him and how she evaluated her approach:

**How she asked**
***In a wobbly, hesitant voice:*** 'Since we went to the pub last night, I'd like to go to see that new film at the cinema tonight. We can always go for a drink afterwards if you want. Is that OK with you?'

**Three good things**
**1.** She spoke out for what she wanted.
**2.** She was respectful of what he wanted.
**3.** She found a compromise.

**One thing she would do differently**
Next time, she would use a firmer, yet kind, tone.

This technique helps you to be more objective, to build on what is good so you repeat it next time, and to keep evolving. This is energizing. To fail to evolve is akin to taking your battery out and letting yourself wind down so that you become a shadow of your potentiality. This is not to say that you will never learn from what goes right, but there is a very strong likelihood that the most powerful opportunities for growth lie in the occasions when things don't go according to plan.

## Learning from setbacks

Too often, however, people learn negative lessons from negative experiences. Let's take a couple of examples.

### GARY'S STORY

Gary's boss told him that he couldn't have the time off he requested because of a looming deadline.

**NEGATIVE LEARNING**

Gary came to the conclusion that his boss didn't like him and that he would never get on in his career. He was personalizing things. This is a common mistake and is often completely unfounded. It also places him firmly in Victim mode (see the drama triangle described in Chapter 2).

**POSITIVE LEARNING**

To get the positive learning, it helps to move into Creator mode (see the empowerment dynamic described in Chapter 2) and use the situation from a learning perspective. This simply requires a decision to see things from another angle. If this is challenging, it is quite useful to think what someone else – someone with a different perspective to yours – might think. It needs to be someone who is positive and wise and deals with situations with relative ease. In doing so, this brings into play a different part of your mind – your higher self, which is compassionate, wise and balanced. Then Gary could have made the pragmatic observation that in business deadlines were important and been able to see the bigger picture:

- He could have looked at why the deadline was looming with work still to be done.

- Had it slipped into a forest of other tasks?

- Had someone dropped the ball?

- Had appropriate priorities been set?

- Was it because someone else had failed to plan and it now fell upon him to catch up?

- Had he set realistic expectations?

- Had he delegated to the right person with clear timelines to be achieved?

- Had he forgotten that the person tasked with doing the job was off sick and no one had picked it up?

The point of this exercise is not to apportion blame but to look at a) what can be done now to resolve the situation and b) what could be done differently next time (the learning).

Of course, a deadline in itself is not the most important thing. It is the consequence of missing it which is more important. Was a more important priority achieved in favour of this one? How important is this customer to achieving the quarterly results? If this customer is the only assurance of achieving the target, then clearly it's an issue that needs to be dealt with immediately. If it is a case of best practice and other, even more important customers are more strategic to results, perhaps the right priorities were set but expectations were mismanaged?

He might also have observed that his boss was under a lot of pressure because, if this deal didn't go through, there were redundancies on the table. He could have chosen to learn that timing is everything and that a 'no' is not a rejection of him but perhaps more about the circumstances, the manner of asking or the timing.

This approach enabled Gary to deal with the situation resourcefully, strategically and practically. His energy transformed from the slump of setback to the power of evolving – learning from the experience.

## SARAH'S STORY

Sarah was a project manager for a building company. Her role was to allocate resources, roles and responsibilities and ensure that projects were delivered on time and within budget.

Increasingly, her job became reliant on technology. There were fewer meetings and more emails; the project management software kept her informed of anything outstanding. However, there were a lot of projects and a lot of tasks and people to keep her eye on. That was OK because she was a good multitasker.

One of the projects was a new-build of an office block. She thought everything was going to plan until the client called and asked where the delivery of washroom fittings had gone – plumbers were ready but they had nothing to work with. Taken off guard, she promised to come back to the client as soon as she had found out what had happened. It turned out that someone she had emailed to order the materials had not received her email and so the order was not placed.

**NEGATIVE LEARNING**

Straight into Victim mode, Sarah's negative learning was that you couldn't rely on technology and that things were easier when you had meetings and communicated directly with them. This left her feeling frustrated and resentful, two qualities that stifle energy.

**POSITIVE LEARNING**

In a different frame of mind, Sarah might have concluded that it always serves to follow up emails and not to mark anything as done until it is confirmed. In this way, it would have shown up as outstanding and she would have been able to resolve the problem before she had three builders waiting for a delivery that wasn't going to arrive. This approach would help her hone her project management skills, not leaving anything to chance. Because things happen despite our best efforts, a good project manager will never trust that something is being done without double-checking that everything is in order.

Learning is energizing. Insights are energizing. Guilt and blame only serve to deplete your energy resources as you spend your limited reserves on covering your back or feeling bad. Out of challenge comes growth. I like to think that life happens *for* you rather than *to* you. This moves you out of

Victim mode and into being curious about what the silver lining is to each cloud.

It may be as simple as developing a sense of humour to get you through the tough times.

......

# 'LIFE IS TOO IMPORTANT TO BE TAKEN SERIOUSLY.'

......

*Oscar Wilde*

Whatever learning you take from any given situation, make sure it's empowering, so that you can evolve to be the best version of yourself.

The lovely poem below helps to illustrate the importance of evolving.

### Autobiography in Five Short Chapters

I

I walk down the street.

There is a deep hole in the sidewalk.

I fall in.

I am lost ... I am hopeless.

It isn't my fault.

It takes forever to find a way out.

II

I walk down the same street.

There is a deep hole in the sidewalk.

I pretend I don't see it.

I fall in again.

I can't believe I'm in the same place.

But it isn't my fault.

It still takes a long time to get out.

III

I walk down the same street.

There is a deep hole in the sidewalk.

I see it is there.

I still fall in ... it's a habit.

My eyes are open.

I know where I am.

It is my fault.

I get out immediately.

IV

I walk down the same street.

There is a deep hole in the sidewalk.

I walk around it.

V

I walk down another street.

*Portia Nelson*

There is something hugely empowering in seeing your own contribution to a problem and taking the positive learning from it. We always have choices. We can live a life of fault-less victimhood, or we can live the life of empowered Creator, constantly evolving and growing. This is the difference between problem-centred living and solution-centred living, between stagnation and progression.

## Time to reflect

1. What negative lessons have you learned from negative experiences?

2. What positive lessons could you learn instead?

3. How does this positive learning affect your motivation and energy?

4. What assumptions do you make that there are alternative interpretations for?

5. For each assumption, think of three alternative interpretations and evaluate the likelihood of each.

# 4
# RESTORERS AND DEPLETERS

• • • • • •

**Understanding and managing
your energy friends and foes**

••••••

Restorers and depleters – or radiators and drains, as they are also called – are those activities or people that either energize you or act as energy vampires. Since everyone is different, we will all have different restorers and depleters: what could energize one person may drain another. This is particularly true for extraverts and introverts. An extravert gets energy from being with people. Left alone too long, they may even feel a little depressed; they will almost certainly feel fatigued. An introvert, by contrast, needs time alone to recharge their batteries. Too many people and too much noise will seem overwhelming to them and they will need to withdraw to get back into balance.

But restorers and depleters aren't only to do with whether or not you are an extravert or an introvert. They can be much more subjective. For example, an energizer for me is being out in nature with my dog. If I feel tired from working too hard, my brain has become foggy or I feel fed up, taking him out for a walk nearly always has a positive effect. Being playful with him has a positive effect, too. He is an antidote to stress for me and it only takes a few minutes to restore myself.

Another energizer is taking a book into a café and reading for a little while. It's like pressing the 'pause' button or taking a break from your day. Another restorer for me is in completing a project or crossing something off my to-do list. It feels very empowering, energizing and restorative to have that sense of achievement and completion. Often, it's completely disproportionate to the actual result! But I enjoy it anyway.

In contrast, a depleter for me – something that puts my energy almost literally on the floor – is phoning a call centre. I find it very frustrating. Maybe it's because I used to hire people for a global leader in the field. It doesn't matter why. It drives me crazy. First of all, there are the interminable instructions for number selections, and then there is the intrusive advertising you have to listen to while you are holding – you are a captive audience, after all. This is topped only by my perception of the complete lack of interest the person on the other end of the phone has in helping me. Just the idea of calling a call centre is enough to have me folding in on myself, but I can't avoid them entirely, so this is where I use my 'secret weapon': the 'energy sandwich'. It's less a weapon than a strategy, and if I forget it I pay the price. But when I remember it, I reap the rewards.

`AN ENERGIZER FOR ME IS BEING
OUT IN NATURE WITH MY DOG.
IF I FEEL TIRED FROM WORKING
TOO HARD, MY BRAIN HAS BECOME
FOGGY OR I FEEL FED UP, TAKING
HIM OUT FOR A WALK NEARLY
ALWAYS HAS A POSITIVE EFFECT.
BEING PLAYFUL WITH HIM HAS A
POSITIVE EFFECT, TOO. HE IS
AN ANTIDOTE TO STRESS FOR
ME AND IT ONLY TAKES A FEW
MINUTES TO RESTORE MYSELF.´

# Using the energy sandwich

The key to restorers and depleters is, wherever possible, to either minimize or delegate your depleters. Usually, when I phone a call centre, it is when I have a problem that I have been battling for a while on my own. This means that my positive energy will already have been eroded to some degree, and maybe completely. In order not to erode it further or risk a negative interaction (which has resulted in the operator putting the phone down on me on more than one occasion), I manage my state with an energy sandwich, which helps me cope with the negative experience more resourcefully. This sandwich has nothing to do with eating and everything to do with being able to manage energy by placing a restorer either side of a depleter, so you eradicate or reduce the negative effects.

My best energy sandwich for the call-centre scenario is to do a round of the emotional freedom technique (EFT) before making the call (this technique is quick to learn and easy to apply; see Appendix I for the instructions). EFT gives me a calm, resourceful energy so that, no matter what happens on the other end of the line, I am less bothered by it and more in control of the situation. After the call, if I am working from home, I will take a few minutes out to play with my dog. This gives me a joyful, light energy, which neutralizes any residual negativity from the call. It also creates a good foundation for me to continue with my day. Undertaking these activities either side of my call centre 'adventure' means that I can enjoy the rest of my day.

Let's take an example of one of my clients. Claire is a manager in a haulage company. She loves managing her team, developing strategy and meeting clients. She dislikes intensely the monthly reports she has to write for the management meetings. It requires a lot of detailed work, which is not her natural talent, though she can do it when she focuses. It just makes her feel as if she is wading through treacle in a straitjacket and concrete boots. It can't be avoided and it can't be delegated, so it is down to her, whether she likes it or not. So she uses her version of the energy sandwich. She preloads her energy with a half-hour meeting with her team on a project that is going well. The positive energy of the team and the progress being made fills her with excitement and contentment, giving her just what she needs to get the report done (the filling to her sandwich). She then moves on to the third part of the sandwich (the second layer of bread) – doing something positive which leaves her with good reserves of energy again. For her, this is having a coffee with a colleague and a catch-up.

**ENERGY RESTORERS**
What works for one person will not necessarily work for someone else and you might also want to try different things depending on where you are, what you're doing and what's available. So, what can go on your restorers list? Here are some popular ones:

- EFT (see Appendix I)
- A conversation with a friend
- Finishing off a job
- Doing some artwork
- Speaking to someone who makes you laugh
- Walking in nature
- Having a coffee break
- Finishing the ironing (is it just me?)
- Finding a nice gift for someone
- Playing with the dog/cat/goldfish
- Doing a puzzle
- Buying yourself some flowers
- Listening to some calming or energizing music, depending on your needs
- Engaging in some mindfulness (more on this in Chapter 7)
- Treating yourself to a delicious lunch

It is so personal that only you can decide what works for you. If you prepare a list, you have it there with you whenever you need it. In this way, you don't have to come up with ideas when you are already depleted – as you know, the brain doesn't perform at its best when it's tired.

# Is your job a depleter?

It's important to understand that the job you do must play to your strengths if it is to work well for you. I do a number of psychometric profiles to help people understand themselves better; one of them (Talent Dynamics) identifies four main styles. Of course, we are more complex than that but it is a good starting point. In playing to your strengths, you can be more productive and energized.

Here are the four main styles:

| Style | Characteristics |
|-------|-----------------|
| Dynamo | • Creative, competitive and target-driven<br><br>• Likes a role where they feel significant and are free to make decisions<br><br>• Great at getting things started; less good at getting them finished |
| Blaze | • Very sociable and talkative; builds strong relationships<br><br>• Enjoys variety but can appear disorganized<br><br>• Easily distracted |

| Style | Characteristics |
|-------|-----------------|
| Tempo | • Good team worker<br><br>• Great at getting things done, though they tend to take their time<br><br>• Likes to be given direction |
| Steel | • Analytical and meticulous<br><br>• Prefers an environment with predictability and strong systems<br><br>• Great with detail but not so good at starting new things. |

There are also nine subcategories. Belbin is another useful tool, again with nine different categories to help you understand what your specific strengths are. If you are someone who likes direction and certainty but works in a creative environment where you are expected to set your own path, with the goals changing on a regular basis, you are likely to feel exhausted at the end of each day.

To take another example, Sam was a really outgoing university graduate. He achieved a 2:1 in Business Studies and he accepted his first job offer as a trainee accountant. He was three months in and knew that he had made a mistake. The office was very quiet, his fellow team-members were not up for sharing a joke or what they had done for the weekend, and the relentless number crunching was mind-numbing. The only light relief was the boss's PA, to whom he often chatted at the coffee machine before being called back to his desk. Sam is a Blaze doing the job of a Steel. This will never work for him because he is too sociable and easily distracted.

Working against type is depleting. Working to your strengths creates flow and energy and you are more likely to be successful as well as happy.

# Time to reflect

1. What are your restorers?

2. How can you ensure more of these?

3. What are your depleters?

4. How can you reduce or eliminate these?

5. What would an 'energy sandwich' be for you?

6. Is your job playing to your strengths? If not, what kind of job would?

# 5

# GOALS AND PRIORITIES

• • • • • •

**The importance of focus for sustainable energy**

• • • • • •

I'm not a huge fan of football, but most of us understand the concept of two teams of eleven men, each trying to get a ball into the competition's net while blocking them from doing the same to your net. Without touching the ball with your hands. Unless it is a ... wait, I'm getting into too much depth here. The point is that the goal is when you get the little ball into the right net following certain rules. And the team with the most goals wins.

But how does this relate to your own life? Footballers spend all their time training to achieve this, day in, day out. They have a manager, they have a coach, they have physiotherapists and they train like crazy. They talk about strategy. They look at the competition and figure out the best way of getting a positive result. They have their eye on the ball every minute of every waking hour. Pun intended. And if they do really well, they can earn untold riches. Because they train and train and train.

The same is true in life. When you are clear about what you want to achieve, focus all your efforts into it, understand any blocks which might stand in your way and create a strategy to deal with them, goals become attainable rather than a wish or desire that reminds you of the discrepancy between being where you want to be and where you are now. When you have a clear goal, it focuses your energy in the right direction, helping you to see the big picture, unburdened by the clutter of life and endless tasks and demands, which pull on your time. It is like a fog lifting; suddenly things are clearer. When the goal is linked to your values and your purpose in life it can help you to transcend stress; it motivates and it galvanizes. Goals don't mean that you can't accommodate unexpected priorities; what it does is clarify your priorities for you.

......

# 'WHEN YOU HAVE A CLEAR GOAL, IT FOCUSES YOUR ENERGY IN THE RIGHT DIRECTION.'

......

I am often asked how I get so much done, how come I am always so motivated. I am going to share my two best weapons here. My clients soon see their results soar when they practise these. This is matched only by an increase in their energy.

There are two main types of goal: time management goals and life goals.

## Time management goals

We all have exactly the same amount of time – 168 hours a week – yet some people achieve far more than others. Having coached hundreds of people in this field, I have found that there are some fundamental differences between the achievers and non-achievers.

I recently had a conversation with some friends where we discussed the concept of commitment. One friend said that he didn't know why he hadn't made it as a well-known speaker yet. It was his life's dream but it wasn't happening for him. I know that he has a lot of personal commitments that draw on his time and he has hobbies which are time-consuming – his golfing takes a good two half-days out of his week plus the socializing which always follows it, for example. In addition, he was decorating his son's house because his son couldn't afford a decorator and didn't know how to do it himself. He loved tinkering about with his motorbike, which took at least half a day a week, and then he would want to take it out for a good run. And then there was his day job. I asked how committed he was to his dream and he got cross, saying he was *very* committed. When I asked how his commitment showed up in his life, he realized that his commitment was really his *desire* for the goal. He was putting in about 15 minutes' effort a week – significantly less than for his golf, his decorating and his bike.

True commitment is desire matched by action. It means pursuing a goal when the original motivation for it has faded. Realizing this was an 'Aha' moment for him. He needed to decide whether he really wanted the goal or not and what he was willing to do to achieve it. Achieving a goal requires effort, prioritization and persistence.

**THE THREE THINGS TECHNIQUE**

There are many time management techniques (see my book *21 Ways and 21 Days to the Life You Want*) but here is one simple technique that will make all the difference in your productivity.

Every morning, decide on three things, and only three things, which you want to complete that day. They might be three small tasks or portions of a much larger task. Make sure you don't have three huge tasks which will leave you feeling daunted and can lead to procrastination. For example, in writing this book I might have as one of my goals drafting a chapter or researching a particular topic. Those are examples of sub-goals of the much larger goal of finishing the whole book and are achievable given the context of my working day. Notice I use the word 'draft', so it doesn't have to be perfect – that will come later. However, it will take a sizeable chunk of the day.

- Another goal might be to pay outstanding bills, which will probably take 5–10 minutes.

- Another goal might be to organize a cupboard which has become dishevelled. That will probably take around 20 minutes.

The golfing friend I mentioned made sure that at least one of his tasks every day was moving him towards his life's dream.

Often, we simply focus on things that are neither urgent nor important and this disperses our energies significantly. Lack of prioritization and procrastination are two of the biggest enemies of effective time management.

This technique enables you to prioritize effectively and gives you a sense of achievement when you have done what you set out to do. Goals need to be feasible in order to be motivating. They also need to be stretching, to give you a sense of satisfaction and provide you with the energy and fuel to keep you on track.

Now, this small to-do list doesn't mean you will not do anything else. Of course, you will answer the phone and do other little chores throughout the day which will fill in gaps, but the three you set out to achieve in the morning will absolutely be your priority and will give you a sense of momentum. It may well be that in completing these three tasks you have plenty of time to undertake other tasks – in which case, go for it. Or take yourself off for a coffee with a friend as a reward.

This technique allows you to focus your energies on the tasks in hand without feeling overwhelmed, which can be an energy vampire. It also gives you excellent clarity of thought.

In deciding on your priorities, do use Stephen Covey's time management grid – it really helps you cut through what is important. Here it is:

|  | Urgent | Not urgent |
|---|---|---|
| **Important** | Quadrant 1<br>Crises<br>Deadlines | Quadrant 2<br>Planning<br>Working towards goals<br>Preparation<br>Prevention<br>Building/ maintaining relationships |
| **Not important** | Quadrant 3<br>Interruptions like some phone calls, emails and texts<br>Some meetings | Quadrant 4<br>Most TV<br>Junk mail<br>Spam<br>Gossip |

**Quadrant 1** – These mission-critical tasks get in the way of results and can be reputation spoilers.

**Quadrant 2** – Though not urgent, the fact that these tasks create your future makes them important. The trouble is that they are the very ones we tend to put off as we get on with the 'great pretenders' – those non-urgent, non-important activities that eat into your day.

**Quadrant 3** – These are the 'great pretenders'; they may make you feel as if you are caught in busy-ness, but they produce few, if any, results.

**Quadrant 4** – This is where a lot of people's energy is wasted. Neither urgent nor important, these activities are just a lot of mind clutter, which gets you nowhere.

When you determine what's really important to your results, you can more easily choose your top three tasks for the day and notice how this affects your results – and your energy.

# Life goals

The other type of goal is a life goal. This is your purpose in life. When you are connected to your purpose, you feel a natural sense of energy. It carries you forward when things get tough. It is a reminder to you of what your life is really about, so that the small things don't become the big things and the big things are valued. If you feel aimless or lost, your purpose will fill that emptiness. This will not only give you a sense of meaning, but it often gives you a deeper sense of connection – to yourself, to others and to the world. Many people, however, are unclear about their purpose or are living a life that is not respectful of it.

Here's another reason why life goals are important. We tend to spend much of our time in the pursuit of pleasure. What's so bad about that, you might ask? Nothing of itself, but if that's your main focus you are missing the importance of two greater sources of happiness. The first is satisfaction, which comes when you have worked hard at something, especially if it was not something for which success was assured – like passing an exam, for example.

The second is fulfilment. This is the kind of happiness you get when you are living your life with purpose, making a contribution to something bigger than yourself. Many of us seek happiness through the pursuit of pleasure, but real happiness only comes when you work on the big stuff. Most people muddle through not knowing what their life's purpose is. They may fall into a career or decide only to do something they know they cannot fail at. When they look back on their lives they realize that they spent far too much time working and not nearly enough time with the ones they loved, doing the things that brought them joy. The result is a life unfulfilled, a life lived on the sluggish end of the energy continuum. This is because living life to someone else's tune, lurching from one task to another and punctuating it with moments of transient pleasure eats away at your energy reserves. If you want to get your mojo back, this is what can help you do it. Since none of us knows how much time we have on this planet, the best way to make the most of it is to be clear about our purpose.

And the great news is that your life's purpose doesn't have to be grand. You don't have to save the world. But it does need to feel significant to your life. It needs to make you feel that your life was worth something to someone.

· · · · · ·

'LIVING LIFE TO SOMEONE ELSE'S TUNE, LURCHING FROM ONE TASK TO ANOTHER AND PUNCTUATING IT WITH MOMENTS OF TRANSIENT PLEASURE EATS AWAY AT YOUR ENERGY RESERVES.'

· · · · · ·

**FIND YOUR LIFE'S PURPOSE**

Here are some examples, but they are only examples. You have to find something that is right for you. And you have to be comfortable with failure because anything that is really worth-while will involve mistakes along the way, disapproval from some and even sabotage from others. And it will need commitment from you. The reward is an animated existence and a legacy you are proud of.

- Make sure my children grow up to be happy, confident, independent and feeling loved.

- Teach one person how to feel good about themselves.

- Create beautiful photographs that are appreciated by the public/my family/my friends/the world.

- Make lots of happy memories for my family.

- Help disadvantaged people find fulfilling careers.

- Support one homeless person to reconnect with society.

- Build a school in Outer Mongolia.

- Raise funds for [your favourite charity].

- Become enlightened (this one is *huge*).

- Create a programme for bullies to help them form empathic relationships with others and give them confidence.

- Be an artist whose work is displayed at Tate Modern.

- Teach people the art of forgiveness, so the world can be a better place.

- Play tennis at Wimbledon.

- Help my clients be the best they can be.

A good way to focus your mind is to think about what you would want to spend your time doing if you knew you had just 12 months left to live. This should help to show you what's really important to you, but if you come up with a list of material things, you'll need to look again at the difference between pleasure, achievement and fulfilment.

Someone I know who is going through bereavement at the moment is spending a lot of money on things because he thinks it will make him feel better. He's in a job he hates. He's lost the woman he loves. And he thinks he will feel good by buying things he likes. Of course, it doesn't work – apart from the 60 seconds following the purchase, or a bit longer if he's lucky. But it's a distraction. Grief is complicated and he needs to work it through. When he's ready, he will feel a lot better if he focuses on his purpose again.

> Since none of us knows how much time we have on this planet, the best way to make the most of it is to be clear about our purpose.

What do you want people to say about you after you leave this planet? That you managed to get to level 150 of the latest video game or that you have a collection of 250 shoes? Or that you could down a pint more quickly than anyone else? When you focus your mind on what you want people to say, it can help you to clarify your purpose more easily. They need to honour your values, which are those things that are important to you.

## WHAT ARE YOUR VALUES?

Here is a selection of values to give you some ideas for your own:

| | | | |
|---|---|---|---|
| Achievement | Adventure | Career | Challenge |
| Comfort | Compassion | Duty | Excitement |
| Fairness | Family | Flexibility | Friendship |
| Freedom | Fun | Happiness | Health |
| Honesty | Humour | Independence | Integrity |
| Intimacy | Joy | Kindness | Learning |
| Love | Making a | Money | Order |
| Being part | difference | Passion | Peace |
| of a team | Power | Recognition | Reliability |
| Positivity | Responsibility | Risk | Routine |
| Respect | Security | Stability | Spirituality |
| Safety | Success | Trust | Travel |
| Support | Variety | Working alone | |

Having a clear purpose inspires action, galvanizes your efforts and creates a positive energy, which fuels you during the most testing of times. Having it honour your values, too, ensures that any internal resistance is minimized.

## FROM YOUR PURPOSE TO YOUR GOAL

In my book *21 Ways*, I talk about how to define your purpose and give an example of Sarah, whose goal is a little more complex:

*'To use my people skills in a job which allows me to make a
real difference to the quality of life of other people, where I
can be a positive example to others of work-life balance, so
that I can connect in a meaningful way with my husband and
friends, bringing fun into my own life and the lives of others.'*

By acting as the guiding principle to everything she does,
this goal will enable Sarah to ensure that she has a fulfilling life. She can ask 'Am I on track? Do I need to adjust my
course? Does what I'm doing honour my values?' It is just as
valuable to have a simpler goal, along the lines of 'To raise
a loving family who enjoy many happy memories in their
lives'. The whole point of your life goal is that it inspires *you*
and nobody but you.

Goals need to be stated in the positive (what you want
rather than what you don't want) and should incorporate or
be respectful of your values – what is important to you. For
Sarah this was fun, connectedness and making a difference.

When thinking about work, consider whether your work
is a job, a career or a calling. A job is something you do
every day to get paid. A career is something you commit to
within a specific profession and which provides progression
for you. A calling is something you are absolutely passion-
ate about; if you didn't need the money, you would do it
for free, all day, every day. It is your calling, and it gives you
purpose and fulfilment. It is part of your identity. And the
good news is that you can make a good living from it, too.
You often get clues to your calling in the things you enjoyed

doing as a child – this is certainly true for me and I wonder if it's true for you too?

Your life's purpose will come from your heart rather than your head. It will motivate you and energize you. It will make your heart sing. However, if you decide on a goal that aims for the approval of others, you are not connecting to *your* purpose. No one can decide what is right for you but you.

······

## 'YOU MUST LISTEN TO THE WHISPER WHICH IS HEARD BY YOU ALONE.'

······

*Ralph Waldo Emerson*

## Time to reflect

1. What three goals do you want to focus on today?

2. Is this the best use of your time?

3. Is there something more important you are avoiding?

4. What is your life's purpose?

5. What are your values (make a list)?

6. Are you on track?

7. What adjustments do you need to make?

# 6

# THE POWER OF INNER TALK

......

**What you say to yourself can boost or sap your energy**

•  •  •  •  •  •

Inner talk is what you say to yourself in the privacy of your own mind, but the things we say to ourselves are often energy depleters.

I have an example from one of my clients. While she enjoyed going to the gym, she sometimes found the workout difficult. I discovered that her inner talk at such times was 'This is really difficult' and it was as though her legs were lead weights and she was climbing Everest with a small community attached to her back. After experimenting with her inner dialogue, she found that what worked for her was 'I am light and fit.' This increased her energy and made her feel almost as if she was running on a cloud – so much easier and better for the joints – which made her workout even more enjoyable. And it was all because she changed what she said to herself.

What's interesting about this is that she didn't need to feel at all light and fit when she started saying it. But by repeating it to herself it became true. Be careful what you say to yourself – your mind is always listening. It's important to say only those things that you want your mind to treat as true.

Probably the most common negative statements I hear from my clients are:

- 'This is too difficult.'
- 'I can't do it.'
- 'I don't know how to do it.'
- 'What if it goes wrong?'

Worst of all is saying 'This is just who I am.' Why is this worse than the others? The first four are at the level of skill and capability – both of which can be improved. 'This is just who I am' is at the level of identity which, on the face of it, is much more difficult to change and is also very defeatist.

Ian McDermott and Joseph O'Connor explain the concept of logical levels in their book *Practical NLP for Managers*. This is a hierarchy of change but I also think of it as a level of 'stuckness' and it can help you understand where you are stuck. Let me take an example from their book to help clarify:

| Level | Name | Description | Example |
|-------|------|-------------|---------|
| Level 1 | Environment | The where and when | I can't do that *here* |
| Level 2 | Behaviour | The what | I can't do *that* here |
| Level 3 | Capability | The how | I can't *do* that here |
| Level 4 | Beliefs and values | The why | I *can't* do that here |
| Level 5 | Identity | The who | *I* can't do that here |

You will see that in the examples a different word is italicized at each level:

- For level 1, environment, the word 'here' is in italics. It is not that they cannot do something, it's just that they cannot do whatever it is in that place.

- For level 2, behaviour, the problem is that they don't think it is appropriate to do whatever it is. It is about action.

- For level 3, capability, the stuckness is about not having the skill to do it.

- For level 4, beliefs and values are a judgement about whether 'it' is something you believe to be right or wrong according to your morals and what is important to you.

- For level 5, identity is about who you are as a human being.

If you are stuck at the identity level, it is much more difficult to effect change because it strikes at your very being. For example, if you say to yourself 'I am useless', it is much more negative than 'Oh, I'm not very good at doing that' or even 'I'm useless at that'. The second example implies that there is room for improvement whereas the first implies that it is something that you will never, ever be able to do.

In his book *Outliers*, author Malcolm Gladwell explains that success is less a matter of skill than a matter of practice. He stipulates that anyone can become an expert at something after around 10,000 hours' worth of practice. I think that's a good point but sometimes it is just a matter of not talking about something as if it's your identity. John was referred to me for some coaching. He was an excellent manager but he just couldn't think creatively – an important aspect of his job when there were problems to be solved. He said, 'I'm just not a creative person. I can't think around a problem, it just isn't me.' He was really limiting himself with this label, so I invited him to metaphorically remove the label and just act as though he was creative next time a problem arose. Just that technique on its own made a huge difference to his problem-solving skills. Of course, he needed to develop his creativity a little more but he was no longer blocked. The point is that giving yourself a label can be positive if it is a good one, but will be negative if it isn't.

# 'BE CAREFUL WHAT YOU SAY TO YOURSELF – YOUR MIND IS ALWAYS LISTENING.'

# The power of And and the power of Yet

Coming back to the fitness theme, when I was young I was always the last person to be picked for team games because no one saw me as in any way sporty. Neither did I. I was the least fit member of my family and the least interested in anything active. My 'identity' was of someone not keen on sport of any kind and not good at sport of any kind. I was seen as more studious, with my head buried in one book or another. But somewhere along the line I decided to change this. Why couldn't I be studious *and* fit? Why couldn't I enjoy books *and* play tennis? They aren't mutually exclusive, unless I make them so. You don't have to be stuck in an identity that doesn't suit you, unless you want to be. I can now play tennis. I'm not the best but I haven't put my 10,000 hours in yet.

Another powerful three-letter word is 'yet'. 'I can't do that yet' implies that you could do it with some practice. It acknowledges that learning is a process. It opens a lot more doors than limiting yourself with negative identity labels.

# Thinking patterns

Dr David Burns, a proponent of cognitive behavioural therapy (CBT), identified thinking patterns that form part of our inner-talk landscape. Our thoughts affect how we feel and how we feel affects our energy. Before I introduce you to the patterns, I want to share with you how we deal with all the millions of pieces of information we are subjected to at any one time, through all of our senses. However, our conscious mind can cope with only between five and seven pieces of data at once. So what does it do with the rest of the data? In order to cope with this onslaught, the mind does one of three things: it deletes, distorts or generalizes.

## DELETION

The mind deletes information that it either does not expect or which seems superfluous. However, the mind doesn't always judge this well because it sometimes deletes helpful information. For example, if you are someone who focuses on the negative rather than the positive, you are deleting positives. In a famous experiment by Christopher Chabris and Daniel Simons, six people are playing basketball and you have to count the number of passes between people in white shirts. Around half of the people in the experiment (including me) completely missed the fact that someone dressed in a gorilla suit entered the scene and beat their chest. This is because the conscious mind is kept busy counting and deletes the fact that a gorilla is there because it is too focused on the details. Such is the power of deletion. What are you deleting?

Watch the video at www.theinvisiblegorilla.com/videos.html

**DISTORTION**

The mind also distorts information to fit in with our expectations. This is how optical illusions work. For example, here is a popular one:

# PARIS IN THE
# THE SPRING

If you read 'Paris in the Spring', you are wrong. It actually reads 'Paris in the the Spring'. We just don't expect to see 'the' twice so we delete the second one, completely oblivious to the fact that we've done so. Often this doesn't cause us problems but it can do. For example, it can cause us to take things personally that are not intended as such. When we take things personally we feel bad. When we feel bad, our energy takes a knock.

Tricia Woolfrey

**GENERALIZATION**

This is when we group things together. Statements like 'always', 'never', 'completely', 'all men are...', 'all women are...' tend to be generalizations. For example, if someone has been let down by a couple of people, they may generalize that 'people can't be trusted'. That's clearly a generalization because most people *are* trustworthy.

We create these generalizations through our personality filters, experiences, values and beliefs. But you don't have to be stuck in them. You just need to be aware that they could be happening and where they might be causing you a problem.

**THE MAIN THINKING PATTERNS**

Here are the main thinking patterns, borrowed from my book *Think Positive, Feel Good*:

| Pattern | Description | Example |
|---------|-------------|---------|
| All-or-nothing thinking | Everything is black or white. It ignores the fact that there are often areas of grey in between. | 'This just hasn't worked at all.' In reality, there are probably aspects of it that did work. |
| Jumping to conclusions | Making an interpretation without the facts, or mind reading. | 'She doesn't think I'm doing a good job.' |

| Pattern | Description | Example |
|---|---|---|
| 'Should' statements | Any statement that includes 'must', 'have to', 'got to' or 'should'. Also 'mustn't' and 'shouldn't'. These words act like rules and cause resistance and feelings of failure. | 'I should do this perfectly – nothing else will do.' |
| Personalization | Thinking you are the cause of any event or that something is about you | 'My son's in trouble and it's all my fault.' |
| 'What if' questions | Anticipating the worst outcome | 'What if it all goes wrong?' |

# How self-talk affects your energy

I wonder what self-talk is affecting your energy – emotional and physical. And how could you change it? Here are some ideas:

| Inner talk | Alternative | Effect |
|---|---|---|
| 'This is difficult.' | 'What's my next step?' or 'What can I do to make it easier?' | This engages the creative mind. |

| Inner talk | Alternative | Effect |
|---|---|---|
| 'I can't do it.' | 'I can't do it yet but I can learn.' | This shows that learning is a process. You couldn't walk before you walked for the first time. You couldn't speak before you uttered your first word. Everybody has to start somewhere and practice is the mother of skill. |
| 'I don't know how to do it.' | 'Who can teach me?' or 'How can I learn?' | This moves you into problem solving. |
| 'What if it all goes wrong?' | 'What can I do to make sure it goes well?' | This engages your intellect so that you can build contingencies rather than simply encounter walls. If you are unsure what to do, ask 'What would so-and-so do to make sure it goes well?' This engages a deeper part of the creative mind and usually brings forward ideas you wouldn't get on your own. It can be fun if you think about the people who would be good in a particular scenario – it is as though they are on your board of advisers, there to help you in times of need. |

| Inner talk | Alternative | Effect |
|---|---|---|
| 'This is boring.' | 'What can I enjoy in this?' or 'How can I make this more fun?' | This moves your focus of attention towards the positive rather than the negative and engages your creativity. |
| 'What a horrible person.' | 'I don't like that man, I must get to know him better.' | I can't claim this one – it's a famous quote from Abraham Lincoln and it shifts you from judgement to openness. |
| 'This is just who I am.' | 'This is who I have been. Who do I want to be? What is my first step?' | This allows you to evolve as a person and get out of your rut. Ruts are completely exhausting! Do you want to stay in or get out? It's up to you. |
| 'This just hasn't worked at all.' | 'What three things went well [there will be three!] and what one thing would I do differently?' | This utilizes the 3:1 rule explored in Chapter 3. It helps you to acknowledge the positive and use any negatives constructively. |
| 'She doesn't think I'm doing a good job.' | 'What is the evidence that this is true? What evidence do I have that this is not true?' | We often personalize things because we filter them through a victim lens and delete any positives, which would give a more balanced perspective. Exploring contrary evidence uncovers those. |

| Inner talk | Alternative | Effect |
|---|---|---|
| 'I should do this perfectly – nothing else will do.' | 'I will do the very best I can.' | This is much more expansive and forgiving, nurturing best effort rather than ruling by fear. Remember that perfection is a tyrant. |
| 'My son's in trouble and it's all my fault.' | 'My son's in trouble because he made poor choices.' | This is placing responsibility where it belongs and avoids any engagement with the drama triangle. |

Since the impact on our energy can be huge whether we use positive or negative thinking, you might as well invest your efforts in positive thinking and enjoy the rewards.

······

'WE EITHER MAKE OURSELVES MISERABLE OR WE MAKE OURSELVES STRONG. THE AMOUNT OF WORK IS THE SAME.'

······

*Carlos Castaneda*

## Gratitude and forgiveness

When you cultivate an attitude of gratitude, your energy lifts, filling you with a benevolence that radiates from within and even having a positive effect on those around you.

You probably recognize that feeling when you are having a bad day and think everything is going wrong and the world is against you. On another day you may feel as though the world is your oyster and everything is flowing for you. This is less likely to be a reflection of life itself than it is to be about your attitude to it. By focusing on what you *can* be grateful for, even in times of challenge, you can transform your experience of life and enjoy a gentle energy to filter your life experiences.

A good habit to develop is to keep a gratitude journal with all the things you are grateful for, from the big things to the little things, such as the fact that the barista smiled today, or, driving to work, you had three green lights in a row. An accumulation of small gratitudes can have a big impact.

......

# 'WHEN YOU CULTIVATE AN ATTITUDE OF GRATITUDE, YOUR ENERGY LIFTS.'

......

Forgiveness can be energizing, too. Your inner talk may involve statements such as 'I can't believe he did that' or 'I'm never going to speak to her again.' Holding on to unforgiveness is a heavy weight to carry but many people have hang-ups about forgiving others. I do a lot of forgiveness work with clients and I can tell you that it is liberating because you are no longer carrying around that baggage. One of the reasons people struggle with forgiving someone is because they think the person doesn't deserve forgiveness or because they think that to do so condones the behaviour. It doesn't even mean you have to trust them again (unless it is appropriate to). In fact, forgiveness is something you do for yourself because it changes how you feel inside. The other person doesn't even need to know you've forgiven them.

In his book *Why Kindness is Good for You*, David Hamilton describes research undertaken in 2000 called the HOPE project and, later, the HOPE 2 project. Forgiveness training was given to people in Northern Ireland who had lost family members during the Troubles. As a result, they experienced a significant drop in their pain, anger, stress and depression as well as an increase in their vitality (energy, appetite, sleep patterns and general wellbeing) as a result of doing the forgiveness work.

When you rid yourself of unforgiveness, you feel lighter, freer and more energized. And you need to be rid of it rather than simply suppressing it because that takes a lot of energy. If you spend 80 per cent of your time thinking negative thoughts or suppressing negative emotions, this will affect you 80 per cent of the time. Any energy wasted on negativity, unforgiveness, anger, self-doubt, blame or guilt is like a black hole to your vitality.

The past is history; it doesn't have to define you. You don't have to carry it around with you. Forgiveness opens up the door to a better future because you will have freed yourself from the pain of your past. Wouldn't it be wonderful to be free?

• • • • • •

'FORGIVENESS MEANS
GIVING UP ALL HOPE
OF A BETTER PAST.'

• • • • • •

Jack Kornfield

Masaru Emoto illustrates the power of our words in his book *The Miracle of Water*. Through photographs of water crystals he illustrates the effect that words have and provides convincing evidence that the resonance of the right words can boost our energy, create harmony in relationships and improve our health. He shows the contrasting effect on crystals of the words 'You tried hard' and 'It's hopeless', the first creating a beautiful crystal and the second creating deformity. The resonance (the vehicle through which energy is transmitted) seems to have an unquestionable impact. And this is true for us, too.

We can't completely control our inner talk, but remember that you are not your thoughts. You can be an observer of them rather than an absorber of them. You can notice them and let them go. You can challenge them. You can create new neural pathways in the mind, which will facilitate more positive thinking. And your energy will thank you.

## Time to reflect

1. What self-talk is sapping your energy?
2. What alternative self-talk can you employ?
3. What unforgiveness are you holding on to?
4. Are you ready to let it go?
5. What can you be grateful for?

# 7

# ZEN AND MINDFULNESS

• • • • • •

**How to give yourself a calming energy**

••••••

How much of your day do you spend completely absorbed in the moment – in what you are doing, whom you are with and where you are? Conversely, when you are having fun with friends or family, do you feel guilty that you aren't working or cleaning or clearing out the garage? If you are working, do you feel guilty that you aren't with your family or friends? Do your loved ones complain that your smartphone gets more attention than they do?

We spend much of our time wishing we were somewhere else, doing something else, regretting something else or wishing for something else. We are rarely in the moment.

What does this do to our energy? I have a lovely client who, when she first came to see me, could be described as full of energy. She smiled all the time – a big, beaming smile – no matter what she was talking about. She said everything was fabulous but she spent the whole session tapping her feet, jiggling her legs or jumping from one subject to another, rarely finishing a point. She suffered great stress but smiled through it all. The stress manifested itself in obsessive-compulsive disorder (OCD). She was constantly washing her just-washed hands, cleaning things that didn't need cleaning and straightening things that didn't need straightening. It was getting to the point where leaving the house was a big challenge because of her rituals.

I taught her mindfulness, which is the art of being in the moment, fully present, uncritically. Because she had never been in the moment, she had never been able to enjoy anything 100 per cent or give herself 100 per cent to anything. Even though she felt driven (a form of energy), she was, at the same time, depleted beyond measure but too scared to stop her rituals. She struggled at first but mindfulness enabled her not only to participate fully in our sessions, her feet, legs and mind relaxed, but also to be more productive at work, more engaged socially and overall easier to be around.

Mindfulness is a practice that has been around for thousands of years and has its roots in Buddhist meditation. It isn't a religion but an awareness of what you are doing at a particular moment in time. Mindfulness has therapeutic benefits as it relieves depression and anxiety, both of which have a negative impact on energy levels.

Zen is a form of Buddhism that emphasizes the value of mindfulness and is characterized by your connection to the world and everything in it, without excessive dependence on material possessions or wealth. It is about relishing life's simple pleasures and being able to experience the reality of life fully.

The difference between mindfulness and meditation is simply that meditation is a more formal way of practising mindfulness:

- Meditation may involve focusing on a candle, or a word, or a sound. It may even involve avoiding thought altogether, which is particularly challenging.

- Mindfulness, by contrast, is focusing your mind on whatever it is you are doing in the moment, uncritically.

As I work as a hypnotherapist and teach people self-hypnosis, I am often asked about the difference between mindfulness and hypnosis. Hypnosis can create mindfulness but has the addition of suggestions for your unconscious mind to absorb. It is therefore more active and transformational, enabling the achievement of specific outcomes. However, it requires more effort and time.

And, in case you are wondering, the difference between mindfulness and relaxation is that relaxation is an absence of effort. Mindfulness may *be* relaxing, but it requires discipline and effort to keep the mind focused on the moment. Like training a puppy, you need to keep calling it back to you. If you try to hold it still, it will struggle against you but gentle discipline is what works.

`WE SPEND MUCH OF OUR TIME
WISHING WE WERE SOMEWHERE
ELSE, DOING SOMETHING ELSE,
REGRETTING SOMETHING
ELSE OR WISHING FOR SOMETHING
ELSE. WE ARE RARELY IN THE
MOMENT. WHAT DOES THIS DO
TO OUR ENERGY?´

# The benefits of mindfulness

Apart from giving you a calm energy, mindfulness has many other benefits, physical, mental and spiritual:

**PHYSIOLOGICAL BENEFITS**
- Lowers stress hormones
- Lowers blood pressure
- Strengthens the immune system
- Increases endorphins
- Increases oxytocin
- Aids sleep
- Reduces sensitivity to pain
- Changes your brain

**PSYCHOLOGICAL BENEFITS**
- Reduces stress
- Supports concentration
- Increases emotional stability
- Improves mood
- Quietens your self-critic
- Enhances decision making
- Develops insight and awareness
- Grounds you
- Lessens addictive behaviours
- Gives you greater self-control

**SPIRITUAL BENEFITS**
- Develops compassion
- Increases a sense of connection
- Opens the heart
- Creates a sense of peace
- Helps you enjoy the moment
- Enriches life
- Helps you accept what is
- Connects you to your wise mind
- Connects you to your higher purpose
- Supports inside-out living*

* Inside-out living is the ability to find happiness from within rather than needing everything outside you to be OK to feel OK on the inside.

# Mindfulness in practice

Mindfulness allows you to press the 'pause' button in a stressful world. Here is a really simple exercise that I teach most of my clients:

**1.** Sit somewhere comfortably, where your back is supported, your feet on the floor and your hands by your sides or in your lap.

**2.** With your eyes closed, simply focus on your breath without judgement.

**3.** Simply notice how your breath feels as it moves in and out of your nose – the difference in temperature as you breathe in to the temperature as you breathe out.

**4.** Notice the movement of your chest and your tummy as you breathe in and out. Notice any sound your breath makes.

**5.** If your mind wanders, which it will, simply bring your attention back to your breath.

Do this exercise for two minutes, bringing your attention back to your breath each time it wanders.

Mindfulness is not an absence of thought, but awareness, a noticing. It acknowledges your thoughts rather than attempting to deny them or push them away. Trying to put a lid on your thoughts is exhausting and almost impossible. Thoughts will come and go and you can simply notice them as you bring your attention back to your breath. Don't judge the thoughts, just notice them and bring yourself back to your breath. Treat your thoughts like clouds; they come and go with no effort. Don't engage with them; simply notice them and let them pass.

I have already mentioned my dog, and one of the things I love to do is walk him in a country lane near where I live and enjoy nature and watching him explore and have fun. Sometimes, though, I will be distracted by what I have to do that day, or what I didn't do yesterday that I wished I had done. When I bring myself back to the here and now, my energy automatically softens and lifts. And the wonderful thing is that this energy permeates other areas of my life. It *adds* to other areas rather than takes away from them.

When your emotional or attentional energies are dispersed, it means that you never apply yourself fully, you never enjoy yourself fully, you can never feel truly fulfilled.

Mindfulness is simple but not necessarily easy because it requires a discipline that you may not yet have.

Coming back to the example of the mind being similar to an untrained puppy, bouncing around all over the place and difficult to control, what a puppy needs are three things:

**1.** Patience
**2.** Repetition
**3.** Firmness

Whatever you are doing, if you find your mind wandering off to other things you should or could be doing, simply bring yourself back to the moment. Be patient with yourself. You may need to repeat this many times before you are able to be in the 'now' and to enjoy each new moment of the now, energized. Remember that allowing your mind to jump from one thing to another takes a lot of energy and will be detrimental to your ability to concentrate.

# Mindful emotions

Somehow in life we learn that negative emotions are bad. In fact, they are merely signposts to say there is a problem that needs to be resolved. So, instead of ignoring these negative emotions, understand their underlying message. Negative emotions are the ones that deplete your energy. There are seven main negative emotions: fear, anger, sadness, loneliness, stress, boredom and guilt. Each has something to communicate to you that needs your attention. Let's take them one at a time and in simple terms:

| Emotion | Message |
|---------|---------|
| Fear | I need to feel safe and secure. |
| Anger | I have been wronged and I need to set boundaries. |
| Sadness | I have lost something important to me. |
| Loneliness | I feel a sense of disconnection. |
| Stress | I am overwhelmed. |
| Boredom | I need more fun or challenge. |
| Guilt | I have wronged someone. |

We experience these emotions through our perceptual filters. They may not be a true representation of a situation but they are a true representation of our *perception* of a situation. By being mindful of your emotions and their messages, you can respond appropriately. By appropriately, I mean from a position of strength and expansiveness rather than fear and contraction. It is too easy to withdraw into yourself without dealing with what's going on. While it may be the right thing for you in certain situations, it is often a defence mechanism, which exacerbates the situation, causing the emotion to become stronger and stronger until it is addressed. Otherwise it leads to another emotion:

• **Frustration:** What I'm doing isn't working.
When we ignore our emotions, frustration is the common result. This gives you a twofold upset: the original problem layered with the twin delight of frustration. And there's more. If you still ignore your emotions, they escalate into a much more serious problem:

• **Depression:** I give up. I can't go on.
The risk now is breakdown. Addressing your emotions can therefore lead to the breakthrough you need. Observing your emotions and being responsive to them helps you to move from helplessness into hopefulness and from hopefulness into happiness. And with happiness comes higher energy. Who knew?

But what should you do with those emotions once they have been acknowledged? Well, that's the subject of another book entirely, but here are three strategies that work well:

**1.** Connect with your inner wisdom.

**2.** Be emotion-responsive.

**3.** Use EFT to reduce the negative emotion.

## CONNECT WITH YOUR INNER WISDOM

Connecting with your inner wisdom enables you to change your initial perception of a situation, or at least to expand it. To connect with your inner wisdom, ask your higher self – that compassionate, wise and balanced self – what it needs right now. The wise mind will always be positive, empowering and kind. It doesn't judge. It doesn't blame. It doesn't make you a victim. It doesn't make you a persecutor. It is your own coach, using challenges to teach you, to elevate you, to strengthen you. It is always working for your benefit, for your highest good. Here are some examples of how you might do this:

| Emotion | Inner wisdom |
|---------|--------------|
| Fear | I understand that fear is just a feeling and it will pass. |
| Anger | I am kindly assertive and I set clear boundaries, teaching people how to treat me all the time. |
| Sadness | Rather than being sad at the loss, I smile at the memory. |

| Emotion | Message |
|---------|---------|
| Loneliness | I can reconnect with people I care about. (Often, though, loneliness starts with feeling disconnected from yourself, so start by connecting with who you are.) |
| Stress | I can change my perceptions of the situation and my priorities, delegate and say 'no' more. |
| Boredom | I can find meaning in what I am doing, or I can do something more fun and/or challenging. |
| Guilt | I can make amends, either directly with the person I wronged, or indirectly by doing good elsewhere. |

......
# `THE WISE MIND WILL ALWAYS BE POSITIVE, EMPOWERING AND KIND .´
......

**BE EMOTION-RESPONSIVE**

Being emotion-*responsive* is all about doing what your inner wisdom needs you to do rather than *reacting* to emotions – which involves either acting them out or suppressing them in ways that are not beneficial to your highest good. The first step is always to connect with your inner wisdom – not your fear, not your ego, not your desire to please, not your comfort zone – just with that part of you which has your best interests at heart, which gives you the long-term ability to help you evolve as you were designed to do.

Remember that your emotions are there for a reason, so acknowledge them and become emotion-responsive (mindfully doing what is needed), rather than emotion-reactive (thoughtlessly suppressing, distracting yourself from or inappropriately expressing emotions).

### USE EFT

The emotional freedom technique, or EFT, is a wonderful way of helping you reduce the emotional charge of a situation. It doesn't alter what happened but it makes it less painful and helps to make you more resourceful so that you can deal with it more effectively. Full instructions for using this empowering technique are given in Appendix I.

> Being mindful of your emotions can save you not only from burning a lot of energy suppressing them, but also the burden of escalating problems, which can lead to burnout or even breakdown.

# Time to reflect

1. Do you apply yourself fully to whatever you are doing in the moment? At work? At rest? At play?

2. Where is your mind when you are at work?

3. Where is your mind when you are enjoying yourself?

4. Where is your mind when you are relaxing?

5. Where is your mind when you are with your family?

When your attention is dispersed, bring yourself back to the 'now'. Do not use this as an excuse to procrastinate, though, but to apply yourself fully to whatever you are doing.

# 8

# EXERCISE AND NUTRITION

• • • • • • •

**The building blocks
of good energy**

• • • • • •

Getting the right exercise and nutrition is an essential part of your energy strategy. In this chapter we will look at the biological side of energy, from exercise to food intolerances and on to hydration, breathing, physiology and nutrition.

We live in such a pressured world, with many demands placed upon us from all directions, that it can be all too easy to overlook the importance of exercise and nutrition. Both need thought and planning but the benefits are enormous, so it is vital to start making these a priority in your life.

Our 'have to have it now' culture has really stood in the way of healthy eating. We have fast-food outlets everywhere. I live in a small village with a population of around 7,700 and we have three Indian takeaways/restaurants, three Chinese takeaways, three kebab shops, one fish and chip shop and three cafes – all within a few minutes' walk. It is hard to get anything healthy from any of these outlets and the temptation to take it easy and let someone else do the cooking is huge! We also have a pizza restaurant and three pubs, so home cooking is very easy to avoid. Most of them deliver, too, so exercise can be another casualty of our lifestyle, providing a double blow to our energy levels.

# Exercise and energy

First of all, let's look at how exercise can increase your energy. Often, when we are tired, the last thing we want to do is anything active. Counter-intuitively, a little exercise or activity can actually energize you. An article published in the *Psychological Bulletin* (2006) showed that, in a study involving 6,800 previously sedentary people, more than 90 per cent of them enjoyed more energy and less fatigue as a result of exercise. Not only that, but the results were greater than using a stimulant medication, even in those with chronic illnesses. So healthy exercise is a vital part of your energy plan.

One executive I coached started work early in the morning, took no breaks, worked until late in the evening and then flopped in front of the TV with little or no energy for his wife and children before dozing off to sleep during his favourite show. He felt he was sleepwalking through life (a common complaint among my clients).

A simple plan of health breaks (a walk in the fresh air and a light lunch out), instead of coffee breaks (a stimulant that causes energy dips as well as spikes) and a sandwich at his desk (wheat makes you feel sluggish), made all the difference. He was more productive at work, despite the fact that he was spending at least an hour less at his desk, and he had more energy left at the end of the day to spend quality time with his young children.

Exercise increases oxygen levels in the body, which helps combat fatigue. It also improves muscle tone, which increases endurance. This, in turn, makes you less susceptible to fatigue. But these aren't the only benefits of exercise. Here's a list of benefits to you of incorporating exercise into your day:

1. Reduces fatigue by increasing oxygen levels in the body
2. Increases stamina by improving heart function
3. Burns calories
4. Increases metabolism
5. Enhances brain function by increasing blood flow to the brain
6. Improves general circulation
7. Reduces stress
8. Increases serotonin levels, enhancing mood stability
9. Creates endorphins, the feel-good chemical
10. Helps you feel empowered
11. Helps to stabilize cholesterol
12. Lowers blood pressure
13. Reduces risk of heart disease, diabetes and cancer
14. While you are busy exercising, you can't also be participating in non-healthy activities such as eating junk food, smoking, etc.
15. Toned bodies look better than flabby ones
16. Slows the aging process
17. Eliminates toxins through perspiration
18. Supports the immune system
19. Can be sociable and fun

Of course, too much exercise can have a negative effect, too, so it's worth speaking to your doctor before undertaking any serious exercise programme. Exercise doesn't have to be formal; it can simply be in the form of more activity, which can be great fun. Here are some examples:

| Formal exercise | Informal exercise |
|---|---|
| High-intensity interval training | Walking |
| Aerobics | Dancing |
| Jogging | Gardening |
| Kick-boxing | Cleaning the house |
| Swimming | Washing the car |
| Gym | Cleaning windows |
| Cycling | Walking to the shops |
| Tennis | Taking the stairs instead of the lift |
| Squash | Decorating |
| Skating | Sex |
| Nordic walking | Horse riding |
| Stepping | Relaxing exercise |
| Zumba | Tai chi |
| Spinning | Yoga |
| Skipping | Pilates |

These are just some examples – the options are endless. I've even heard of walking football for those who can't run but enjoy the game and the teamwork. It's good to do different activities so that you don't get bored and also so that your body benefits from the variety. Do remember to do a warm-up and a cool-down so that you prepare your body for exercise and avoid the risk of injury. If in any doubt, you could book yourself a session with a personal trainer who will create an exercise programme to suit you.

Research suggests that taking 10,000 steps a day every day can have a positive impact, so why not invest in a pedometer and set yourself a daily challenge? You could buddy up with someone so that you keep each other on track and provide the necessary motivation.

When you make exercise part of your daily life, you soon see results and you will actually start to look forward to it. Personally, I exercise every day by walking the dog twice, doing 15 minutes of exercises in the morning 90 per cent of the time and also going to the gym. I throw in the odd evening doing a bit of ceroc (jive dancing). I enjoy yoga, too. Sometimes I will do 30 minutes of stepping while I watch a favourite TV programme. I can tell you that when I have convinced myself that I really don't have time, I can feel my energy and productivity dropping and my stress rising. I have found it's worth getting up a little earlier to make the time.

Look for ways of increasing your activity and exercise. If you can do this outdoors, so much the better because daylight is also energizing, even if the sun is hidden behind a few clouds.

If you are one of those people who are too busy to exercise, think about how much time you'll have on your hands if you succumb to illness. Exercise is an investment in yourself, so be selfish with your exercise time. Put it in the diary and make it an appointment with yourself that doesn't get cancelled.

> When you make exercise part of your daily life, you soon see results and you will actually start to look forward to it.

## Nutrition and energy

Not only can the wrong foods deplete your energy (too many carbs and sugars give an quick energy surge and then an energy slump just as quickly) but not having the right foods in your body can also leave you feeling constantly tired. Your body needs a variety of good foods to keep you healthy and strong. You also need water (see below), oxygen (see below) and light (as above).

Our bodily functions do not happen of their own accord, but through a complex system that requires nutrients to help the body perform at its best. Nutrients provide your body with the raw materials it needs to perform optimally, both physically and mentally. However, it is very difficult to get the required daily amounts for vibrant health from food alone because modern farming methods, storage methods, microwaving and overcooking deplete the nutrients in food before we eat it. Added to that, if you have poor digestion, your body will not absorb nutrients as well as it should. Our body needs to be able to absorb the nutrients efficiently so that the benefits of healthy food can be enjoyed.

A healthy diet includes lots of alkaline-forming foods (about 80 per cent) with the remaining 20 per cent from acid-forming foods (see Appendix II). Too much acidity causes not only fatigue but also mineral depletion and it can also lead to serious illnesses, such as cancer.

About half your diet should come from vegetables and fruit. Minimize junk food as much as possible – it might give you an immediate energy rush, but in the long term it robs you of vitality and leads to seesawing energy, which is very unhealthy.

Nutrients fall into two main categories: macronutrients and micronutrients.

**MACRONUTRIENTS**

These include protein, fats, carbohydrates and fibre.

- **Protein**

Protein is made up of amino acids and is necessary to build and repair tissue, make enzymes, hormones and more. The best sources are 'complete proteins', those containing all essential amino acids, and they can be found in meat, hemp-seeds, fish, poultry, eggs, milk products, cheese, soya beans and quinoa (complete protein derived from the seeds of a grain). Whey protein, chlorella, spirulina, goji berries and amaranth are also complete proteins.

- **Fats**

Some fat is essential for health, but it needs to be the right kind of fat. Essential fats are those that the body cannot make itself but that we need to grow, renew and be healthy. They are used in the body to help your body absorb some vitamins; they are required for cells, hormone function, brain health, mood and more. Good sources include oily fish, seeds, nuts, extra virgin olive oil and chia seeds.

- **Carbohydrates**

Carbohydrates come in two main forms: simple and complex. When you are tired, the body tends to crave simple carbs such as white bread, white rice, biscuits, cake and sugar, but while this does cause an immediate spike in energy, it is quickly followed by an energy slump. This makes you crave more and, as carbohydrate turns to fat quickly in the body, can cause weight gain as well as your energy dips. Another reason we crave carbohydrate is because it raises serotonin, which improves mood. However, it is not a good long-term solution to low mood.

Complex carbohydrates, on the other hand, have a more stabilizing effect and help long-term energy. Good sources include wholewheat bread, brown rice, oats, lentils and quinoa.

We often feel bloated after eating carbohydrate because it binds with three molecules of water compared to one for protein. (This is why we appear to lose weight quickly when we remove carbohydrate from our diet, although in fact we are just losing water.) A good balance of complex carbohydrates in our diet will make all the difference.

- **Fibre**

Fibre is a form of carbohydrate that helps stabilize blood sugar and energy, and lower cholesterol. Fibre is essential for keeping you regular: people often feel sluggish if their bowels are sluggish. Good sources of fibre include brown rice, pulses, quinoa, potato skins, fruit (unless you juice the fruit and remove all the fibre) and whole grains.

**MICRONUTRIENTS**

These are all the vitamins and minerals required by the body which help brain function, the immune system, skin tone and elasticity, hair strength and thickness and, of course, your energy.

The recommended daily allowance (RDA) of a nutrient, often quoted on food packaging, is the absolute minimum required for life. The optimum daily allowance (ODA) is rarely quoted but this is what provides therapeutic levels for health and energy.

Dr James F. Balch says that 'a deficiency of a vitamin or mineral will cause a body part to malfunction and eventually break down – and, like dominos, other body parts will follow.' Healthy food is medicine. It's also delicious and doesn't need to take a long time to prepare, just planning. My clients find my meal planner useful for this as it also has information on how to get your RDA, how to understand portion sizes, a list of foods that supply specific nutrients and a short guide to the glycaemic index to help stabilize your blood sugar, as well as some meal ideas.

The most important micronutrients for energy are magnesium and iron.

- **Magnesium**

Magnesium improves your core energy and is found in many foods. However, because of the way our food is farmed, the levels are not as high as they were years ago, so it is more difficult to get the levels your body needs by food alone. You might need it as part of a good supplement programme if you are particularly tired and stressed. Here is a list of magnesium-rich foods:

| | | | |
|---|---|---|---|
| Almonds | Aubergines | Apples | Brazil nuts |
| Broccoli | Blackberries | Cashews | Peanuts |
| Chicken | Crab | Cheddar cheese | Milk |
| Cabbage | Carrots | Celery | Fresh peas |
| Garlic | Green beans | Mushrooms | Lettuce |
| Onions | Parsley | Sweetcorn | Tomatoes |
| Prunes | Dried apricots | Dried dates | Dried figs |
| Raisins | Grapes | Green leafy vegetables | Potatoes with skins |

- **Iron**

Iron is also important for energy because it helps transport blood and oxygen around the body. Here are some iron-rich foods:

| | | | |
|---|---|---|---|
| Beef (lean) | Cheddar cheese | Chicken | Cottage cheese |
| Eggs | Lamb | Liver | Pork |
| Salmon | Walnuts | Artichokes | Aubergines |
| Avocado | Broccoli | Carrots | Cauliflower |
| Celery | Mushrooms | Red meat | Fresh peas |
| Potatoes | Red cabbage | Tomatoes | Green leafy veg |
| Brown rice | Currants | Dates | Prunes |
| Figs | Raisins | Apple | Sunflower seeds |
| Bananas | Blackberries | Cherries | Oranges |

## Healthful eating

Health is more than just an absence of symptoms and, to facilitate optimal health, diet is really important. I like to talk about *healthful* eating rather than *healthy* eating. By this I mean having a broad range of all the food groups, in balance. Too many people are malnourished, perhaps because of the over-availability of junk food and the cultural dependence on fast food and quick fixes. The trend for size zero does not help, either. Health and energy require a balanced and comprehensive approach in moderation.

## HOW TO GET YOUR NINE A DAY

The five-a-day goal (five portions of fruit and vegetables a day) is an absolute minimum, not a limit, and you will need a lot more if you are stressed or have any health concerns. Nine a day has been recommended as a healthier and still achievable goal. In his book *Eating Well for Optimum Nutrition*, Andrew Weil recommends the following:

- A banana with a glass of orange juice with your breakfast
- Two cups of salad and some vegetable juice with your lunch
- A cup of broccoli with dinner, with some berries and a slice of melon for dessert

Remember, though, that if you want to avoid the sugar hit, real fruit is better than juice. If you do have juice, make sure you have some protein at the same time, to avoid an energy spike and slump.

Here is my suggestion for a way to get your nine a day:

- Berries in your porridge and an apple to follow (eat the skin for fibre)
- Fresh vegetable soup for lunch and a side salad
- Crudités for snacks
- Ratatouille with your main meal
- Fruit salad for dessert

**THE 80/20 RULE**

I'm a believer in moderation so, as long as you eat health-fully 80 per cent of the time, you should be absolutely fine. If you deny yourself any of the less healthy foods we call treats, then you will tend to crave them or feel deprived, which will make you crave them even more. Just make sure you fill up on healthy foods.

**WHEAT ALTERNATIVES**

Many people find a huge increase in their energy levels if they cut down on wheat, but it can be tricky as wheat is a staple food in our society and appears as an ingredient in many processed foods. Gluten-free items often have a high glycaemic index, which will deplete your energy just as much. Having said that, food outlets are getting really wise to this problem and are starting to offer no-bread options in their sandwich selection.

- **Foods including wheat:** bulgur wheat, sorghum wheat, semolina, couscous, breads, buns, cakes, pasta, scones, pastries, quiche, certain breakfast cereals, wheat starch, baking powder, gravy powder, canned soups and batter.

- **Wheat alternatives:** buckwheat, barley, rye, oats, rice, corn (maize), quinoa, potato, Doves Farm gluten-free flour, spelt flour (most of the time), wheat-free pasta, soda bread, rye bread, rice cakes, oatcakes, corn thins.

**WEANING YOURSELF OFF COFFEE**

One good coffee a day is fine, but if you are relying on it to keep yourself awake, you can anticipate a day of peaks and troughs. It's time to start weaning yourself off. There are a couple of options here. The first is to start reducing the quantity and strength of your coffee until you get down to your one a day.

The second is to choose chicory coffee instead. It has the kick that many people enjoy from conventional coffee, but without the energy slump and with some additional health benefits. Chicory coffee is said to be better for your stress levels, gentler on the liver and good for easing constipation. Of course, there are also other hot drink options, such as green tea, peppermint tea and camomile tea.

**WEANING YOURSELF OFF SUGAR**

As already mentioned, we often crave sugary foods when we are tired because they give us a big energy spike. However, this is soon followed by an energy slump, which has you craving more sugar. If sugar is your energy-enemy, there are two ways of weaning yourself off it. The first involves stabilizing your blood sugar by eating mainly low or medium GI foods.

The way to stabilize your blood sugar levels and break the vicious spike-slump circle is to eat little and often. Three healthy meals a day with two healthy snacks is optimum. The next thing is to remove from your home all foods that give you that energy spike – the white bread, white pasta, biscuits and sweets. You will also need to keep alcohol to a minimum.

Replace your simple carbohydrates with whole foods, which release their energy slowly and so help stabilize your blood sugar. Many whole foods are low on the Glycaemic Index (GI), which is a way of measuring how quickly a food enters the bloodstream and raises blood sugar. These low GI foods are best for maintaining your energy at a stable level throughout the day. Here is a list of these, together with examples of medium GI and high GI foods:

### Low GI foods for long-term energy
- All pulses, e.g. lentils, chickpeas, soya beans, baked beans, kidney beans, butter beans, borlotti beans; barley
- Apples, dried apricots, peaches, plums, cherries, grapefruit, pears
- Avocados, courgettes, spinach, peppers, onions, mushrooms, leafy green vegetables, leeks, broad beans, green beans, sprouts, mange-tout, cauliflower, broccoli
- Natural yoghurt, milk, nuts

### Medium GI foods for medium-term energy
- Sweet potatoes, boiled potatoes, yams, raw carrots, sweetcorn, peas
- All types of wholewheat pasta, oats, porridge, oatmeal biscuits, noodles
- Whole-grain rye bread, pitta, buckwheat, bulgur wheat, brown rice
- Grapes, oranges, kiwi fruit, mangoes, beetroot, fresh dates, figs

**High GI foods for short-term immediate energy**

- Glucose, sugar, honey, pineapple, bananas, raisins, watermelon
- Baked potatoes, mashed potatoes, parsnips, cooked carrots, squash, swede
- Wheat crispbreads, cream crackers, white bread, rice cakes, couscous
- Cornflakes, bran flakes, instant oats, popcorn, muffins, crumpets
- Orange juice, dried fruit

Having said all that, low GI food isn't the full picture. In his book *The Low-GL Diet Bible*, Patrick Holford explains that some low GI foods have such low levels of carbohydrates that their glycaemic load has a detrimental effect on your energy. At the same time, some manufactured foods sold as low GI have high levels of slow-releasing sugars, making them technically low GI but with sufficient quantities of sugar to have a big impact on your energy. It gets complicated and I'm all for the easy life, so if you stick to natural foods in moderate quantities and focus on the low-GI carbohydrates, you should notice a positive difference quite quickly.

The second way to wean yourself off sugar involves altering your taste buds. You may be used to sweet-tasting foods but you can alter your taste buds. If you take sugar in tea and coffee, start to use less and less until you have none at all. Don't replace it with sugar substitutes because they also give you that energy spike and do nothing for altering your taste buds. I have clients who would have had two sugars in their coffee and now can't stand the thought of it just by using this simple technique. You get used to the adjustments very quickly. Here are some more ways to reduce or eliminate the sugar cravings:

- Drink a cup of hot water and lemon before you have anything sweet.

- Brush your teeth before eating.

- Avoid low-calorie versions of sweet food and drinks as they often contain sugar substitutes.

- Dilute fruit juices (high in sugar) with water so they taste less sweet.

- Eat dried fruits, which have a high concentration of sugar, infrequently and in very small quantities.

As a bonus when stabilizing your blood sugar levels, you are likely to lose fat and avoid developing type II diabetes as a result of the dietary changes you make.

**ALCOHOL**
Alcohol is high in sugar and for this reason alone it will reduce your energy levels, quite apart from the sluggishness

you will feel if you drink too much of it. In excess, whether or not you experience a hangover, alcohol will sap your energy by causing dehydration and an electrolyte imbalance.

Alcohol also affects your ability to enjoy restorative sleep. This will, in turn, affect your performance at work and your stress levels. If you find yourself drinking as a way of managing stress, refer to Chapters 3, 6 and 7 and Appendix I in particular, though there are useful tips in the other chapters too.

Drinkaware now says that there is no safe level of alcohol consumption and government guidelines recommend that both men and women drink no more than 14 units a week. That means no more than six 175-ml glasses of wine or six pints of average-strength beer spread evenly across the week.

## HEALTHFUL EATING TIPS

1. Eat little and often – three healthful meals and two small healthy snacks a day. The snacks stabilize blood sugar and mean that you don't crave junk food to increase your energy. Almonds are perfect for this.

2. Make sure around 25 per cent of your calories come from protein and healthy fats, with about two portions of oily fish a week.

3. Eat a rainbow of food – lots of colour means lots of nutrients. Beige food is almost always junk food.

**4.** Aim for a minimum of five fruits and vegetables a day; nine is optimal.

**5.** Buy in season for taste, value and nutritional density.

**6.** Swap simple carbohydrates for complex ones. Simple carbs like white bread, white pasta, white rice, cakes, biscuits, sweets, chips just make you feel sluggish.

**7.** If you must have junk food or simple carbs, do eat some protein at the same time to avoid the energy dip.

**8.** Avoid diet foods and drinks – they give you energy dips too.

**9.** Avoid highly processed foods.

**10.** Lightly cook vegetables or eat raw to preserve nutrients.

**11.** Eat breakfast within two hours of waking.

**12.** It is important to be relaxed when you are eating, to help your body digest the food effectively. This also helps with the acid/alkaline balance (see Appendix II).

**13.** Chew your food 20 times before swallowing, to allow the enzymes to break down the food effectively.

**14.** Drink 30–45 minutes before meals rather than during meals, as this dilutes the gastric juices important for breaking down the food.

**15.** Eliminate any foods to which you are intolerant (see below).

······
### 'EAT A RAINBOW OF FOOD – LOTS OF COLOUR MEANS LOTS OF NUTRIENTS. BEIGE FOOD IS ALMOST ALWAYS JUNK FOOD.'
······

**TAKE SUPPLEMENTS**

If you want to make doubly sure that your nutrition is optimal, do take good supplements. As a base level, the following is recommended:

- A very good, food-state multivitamin and mineral
- Essential fatty acids (krill oil is excellent)
- An antioxidant to protect you from free radicals

Other supplements that might work particularly well for your energy will depend on your individual health profile. You will need to see a qualified nutritionist to have a full consultation to find out what would be right for you. The above is a very good start.

Do bear in mind that all supplements are not created equal. The cheaper high street versions tend to be high on fillers and synthetics, making them difficult for your body to absorb. In addition, they tend to be of quite low potency. Food-state supplements are stronger and can therefore have a bigger impact. Nutrients that are particularly helpful for energy will vary, depending on your individual situation.

## CHECK FOR FOOD INTOLERANCES

Sometimes the kind of food you eat can affect your energy. If you are intolerant to a particular food it can create all kinds of problems, from bloating to poor concentration, loss of motivation, skin problems, panic and fatigue.

There is much confusion about food intolerances because they can cause a wide variety of symptoms. As well as fatigue, a food intolerance may cause IBS, bloating, indigestion, water retention, difficulty losing weight, lack of concentration, poor memory, poor motivation, lack of clarity, depression, flatulence, belching, runny nose, catarrh, hay fever, eczema, asthma, chest infections, cravings, thrush, nail infections, verrucas, warts, skin rashes, PMT, moods, headaches, hyperactivity, palpitations, raised blood pressure, insomnia and nausea. That's quite a list. And, of course, there can be many other causes for these symptoms.

Intolerances are often confused with food allergies but they are completely different. An allergy is a problem with your immune system and the reaction is immediate, severe and life threatening. Common symptoms include hives, swollen tongue, swollen lips and fainting. Even a trace amount can have this effect if you are allergic. Common allergens are shellfish, eggs, milk and peanuts.

A food intolerance, more accurately called a food sensitivity, is a problem with your digestive system. Many people come to me for a food intolerance test as part of my nutritional offering but I don't like doing them in isolation because they are only a symptom of something else. It is much better to know why your body is not tolerating the food(s). In my experience, it is a mixture of gut health and stress. Improve the digestive system, work on the emotional issues and manage stress and your body will thank you.

Eliminating foods to which you are intolerant can reduce symptoms but you don't want to do this for life. It is far better to deal with the cause, so that your body can tolerate all foods in moderation.

People are often surprised to learn that they are not intolerant to a particular food that they seem to react to. This is usually because they are not so much intolerant to the food as that they are overdosing on it. Wheat, a common offender, may show up as OK on the test but because the person is eating it for breakfast (toast), lunch (sandwich) and dinner (pizza) as well as in snacks (biscuits and cake), the body is reacting. The body can't cope with this amount. Simply reducing their wheat intake to once a day or less could make all the difference. Wheat is known to bloat the body, too, so eliminating it can reduce your waistline quite quickly.

Sometimes the problem is toxic load – having too many unhealthy foods at the same time. For example, you might show up as tolerant of wheat, dairy and sugar, so you feel confident to eat these foods. However, if you go out for dinner and have bread while you order, paté and toast for the starter, pasta carbonara for your main course (cheese and cream as well as wheat), ice cream for dessert (sugar, cream and fat) and wash this down with wine (sugar and yeast), your body may just not cope with the onslaught. You feel ill not because of food intolerances but from toxic overload. This is why it's so important to make sure all your meals contain a good variety of healthy foods: balance is key.

While wheat and gluten are common culprits, you can be intolerant to anything but rarely permanently because your body is changing all the time. Keep a food diary to record what you are eating so that when you feel low in energy you can identify any possible causes. A simple food intolerance test (see www.yourhealthuk.com) can quickly identify your food intolerances so that you can eliminate them and replace them with something that will benefit your body. In removing any food from your diet it is important to replace it with something else from the same food group so that you are not missing out on any vital nutrients.

Do bear in mind that common symptoms of food intolerances may actually be an indication of something else. If you have any health concerns, do see your doctor.

# Stay hydrated

We are made up of approximately 70 per cent water. This is essential for digestion, brain function, energy, absorption of nutrients, circulation and elimination of waste. Dr F. Batmanghelidj, author of *Your Body's Many Cries for Water*, even credits this elixir for completely reversing chronic fatigue syndrome.

A good 80 per cent of the people I work with are dehydrated (this shows up when I do a bioenergetics screening). This is either because they do not drink enough water (the obvious cause) or because they are drinking too much tea, coffee or alcohol, which act as diuretics. Sometimes it is because their cells are not allowing their body to absorb the water, which is a more complicated problem.

It is vitally important, not just for your energy, but for your general health and wellbeing, to drink about 2 litres of water daily, not all in one go but spread throughout the day. It's important not to wait until you are thirsty because thirst is a sign that you are already dehydrated. If you drink tea, coffee or alcohol, you need to drink even more water to counteract their diuretic effect. In hot weather or during exercise, you will also need to replace the water lost through perspiration.

Ongoing thirst can also be a sign of diabetes, gall bladder problems, candida or potassium deficiency, so do get checked out by your doctor if you are concerned.

If you suffer from brain fog or fatigue, hydration can make all the difference.

## Breathe deeply

It goes without saying that without breathing you have a much bigger problem than low energy! Most people's breathing is very shallow, which means that their brain is not getting the oxygen it needs to function well and their energy will be compromised.

To keep yourself energized throughout the day, simply make sure that you are breathing deeply into your lungs, holding that breath for a moment and then letting it go slowly. Slow, deep breaths are what you need, so that your chest and abdomen move with the breath. As well as revitalizing you, deep breathing detoxes the body, increases relaxation, improves sleep and balances acidity and alkalinity in the body.

Although largely an unconscious activity, by applying conscious thought to the quality of your breathing, you can improve your health physically and emotionally as well as increasing your energy.

---

### BREATHING ENERGIZER

**1.** Sometimes it's useful to do a specific breathing exercise like this:

**2.** Breathe in and out quickly and sharply ten times.

**3.** Hold your breath for a count of ten.

**4.** Now breathe in deeply, hold for a count of ten and breathe out slowly.

---

## Watch your posture and body language

Sometimes, simply the way you hold yourself can deplete your energy. If you are slumped at the shoulders with your head bowed, it is practically impossible to feel energized, or even positive. A physical slump goes hand in hand with an energy slump. By contrast, if you stand tall, shoulders back, neck nice and long with your head up, eyes looking straight ahead and tummy tucked in, you should feel an increase in your energy immediately. Try smiling too, and notice a subtle shift in the quality of the energy you now enjoy.

We are all a little different, so experiment with changing the way you sit, stand and move around until you get it just right for you.

# Time to reflect

1. Do you exercise regularly?
2. Do you have an active lifestyle or is your sofa your best friend?
3. Are there any foods that seem to cause a slump in your energy?
4. Do you enjoy a healthy, varied diet?
5. Do you take basic nutrients to support your energy and vitality?
6. Do you drink plenty of water throughout the day?
7. Do you breathe well?
8. Does your posture support high energy?

# 9

# REST AND RELAXATION

• • • • • •

The importance of downtime
to create more uptime

• • • • • •

No book about energy would be complete without looking at the need for rest and relaxation to restore your energy and create balance. Good rest and relaxation are my last prescription for good core energy – the kind that enables you to enjoy work, rest and play, gives you balance in your life and in your body, and nurtures the spirit.

## A good night's sleep

First and foremost, every day you need to make sure that you get enough quality sleep for you. Adults need eight hours a night on average but some people need more and some less. Some people find that having too much sleep is a de-energizer, making them feel tired and even groggy. For others, not having enough sleep affects their energy, concentration, humour and health. You will be the best judge of what is right for you.

A sign of a good night's sleep is that you wake feeling refreshed. During your sleep your body repairs and rejuvenates itself, the liver detoxifies and cleanses and your mind reinforces your learning and your memory.

To ensure that you get a good night's sleep, here are some tips:

**1.** As often as possible, go to bed before 11 p.m. After this time your liver is working hard and if you are awake, it won't be doing a good job of detoxing your body. This can be why many people feel sluggish in the morning.

**2.** Avoid eating heavy meals just before going to bed as the digestive process can get in the way of restful sleep.

**3.** Have a consistent sleep/wake schedule. Where possible, have a set time for going to sleep and waking up. That way your body isn't constantly playing catch-up with itself.

**4.** Reduce stimulants, especially coffee, other caffeinated drinks (i.e. tea, cola), alcohol and cigarettes. A small amount of alcohol has a stimulant effect and a large amount has a depressant effect that will disrupt your sleep.

**5.** Limit your exposure to light at night. If necessary, get yourself some blackout curtains.

**6.** Keep your bedroom free of clutter and anything work-related. It should be a calm environment for rest.

**7.** Reduce your exposure to electromagnetic fields (EMFs) from your clock radio, your TV, remote control, DVD, laptop, smartphone, iPod, tablet and chargers, which all emit energy that can interfere with your sleep patterns.

According to Ann Louise Gittleman in her book *Zapped*, your length of exposure to electromagnetic fields means more to your health overall (not just your sleep) than its actual strength. If you have an average of eight hours' sleep a night, this gives you 2,920 hours' exposure a year alone. She cites chronic fatigue as one of the many health problems attributed to exposure to EMFs.

**8.** As exercise acts as a stimulant, make sure you finish exercising at least a couple of hours before you go to bed.

**9.** Enjoy a cup of camomile tea prior to retiring for the night.

**10.** Light reading before bed is a good way to prepare for sleep – but avoid newspapers and work-related material.

**11.** Avoid stressful activities before bed, including discussing emotional issues.

**12.** If you tend to take your problems to bed, write them down before you sleep and then put them aside so you can more easily let go of your day.

**13.** Listen to a hypnotherapy CD or other relaxing CD to ease your mind (my *Sleep Well* MP3 has proved very effective for my clients).

**14.** Do EFT beforehand to prepare your mind for rest (see Appendix I).

# Taking breaks

It is important to take breaks throughout your working day, too, especially if your work is very intense. Ideally, you should have regular complete breaks from your work by going out into the open air or, if that is not possible, at least get away from your desk and/or from what you are doing.

For example, when I am doing a lot of writing, I will stop and do a bit of filing or call a client, or have a cup of liquorice tea (great for your adrenals) or, preferably, take the dog for a walk down the country lane near where I live and where I can enjoy looking at the countryside. If I am running a training course, I will need some quiet time to myself for ten minutes because training is all about giving out and it's a good way of staying fresh throughout the day.

# Using meditation, mindfulness and self-hypnosis

The benefits of meditation and mindfulness are becoming increasingly well known. We covered this in Chapter 7 but it's worth including here as an important part of your rest and relaxation strategy. Self-hypnosis has similar benefits. All these techniques are relaxing:

**Mindfulness,** as we have seen, is a wonderful technique to calm you no matter where you are or what you're doing. It requires you to focus on the present moment, uncritically. Often, with my very stressed clients, I will start a session with just two minutes of mindfulness, focusing on the breath. Two minutes makes a huge difference to their stress levels and energy and is easy to do at any time.

Mindfulness is a non-doing, a way of being, in the moment and present. The technique lets you acknowledge thoughts rather than suppressing them and brings a calm energy to whatever you are doing. You can even clean the house mindfully, cook a meal mindfully, walk mindfully, take a shower mindfully.

**Meditation,** the more formal practice of mindfulness, has benefits for relaxation that are just as good as mindfulness, although some meditation practices require non-thinking, which is more challenging. A meditation is usually done at a particular time of day and often uses an object to focus on, such as a sound or a candle. CDs of guided meditation are available if you prefer to have someone lead you through the process.

**Self-hypnosis**, like mindfulness and meditation, helps to calm nervous energy that can be so exhausting and stressful and instead increases core energy – that sustainable energy that helps you handle stress and the challenges of life more easily. I teach many of my clients a system called An Inside Job™, a cross between self-hypnosis, meditation and mindfulness. It's a great way to instil a calm and resourceful energy as well as emotional resilience. It can also help you create a blueprint for how you want to be in particular situations as well as deal with internal conflict, depending on how you focus your practice.

# Balancing your life load

If you lead a very busy life, even if you are busy doing things you enjoy, your life load may be affecting your energy, so do make sure you have some still, peaceful time, just to be. We spend far too much time as human doings rather than human beings.

The choices we have for rest and relaxation are endless; we just have to choose what suits us. Here are some examples of how some of my clients like to relax:

- Sandy's favourite way of relaxing is reading a book in the garden with a peppermint tea.

- Jim prefers to take his son out for a bike ride by the river.

- Jude has a massage once a week.

- Kevin's favourite way to shut out the world and his worries is to have a swim and a sauna, early in the morning, before most people are awake.

- Jane loves nothing better than a walk in the rain.

- Her husband Carl prefers jogging as a way of getting away from it all and releasing any stress from his day.

- Lisa enjoys a weekly aromatherapy massage.

- Sophie alternates reiki and reflexology to rebalance her energy.

- James loves his weekly tai chi sessions.

Everybody's preferred way of relaxing is different. It is important to find what works for you and to have the right balance of relaxing activities. You will know if the balance is right if your energy is stable, and you feel resourceful and resilient even in times of challenge.

Good-quality rest will not only affect your energy, but also your mood and your health. It also makes you much easier to be around. Do you know anyone who is on the go all the time and never has any downtime? How fun are they? They tend to be very tetchy, intense and exhausting to be with.

## Laughter as medicine

One of the most fun ways of increasing your energy and relaxing is to engage in activities that make you laugh. In his book *Anatomy of an Illness*, Norman Cousins described how he suffered from a serious illness as well as adrenal exhaustion. He was concerned that the medication he was on, though it helped manage his physical symptoms, was having a toxic effect on his body, which manifested itself in hives. He put himself on a diet of Candid Camera and Marx Brothers films and laughed his way out of a crippling disease his doctors thought was irreversible. What a lovely way to be healthy and energized!

## Time to reflect

1. Do you have enough rest and relaxation in your life?
2. What are your favourite ways to relax?
3. How can you introduce more of these into your week?

• • • • • •

# CONCLUSION

You were meant to live life full of energy. But, in this twenty-first-century life, we have so many demands and expectations that many of us are running on empty.

In this book, I have shared with you tools and techniques to help you feel energized so you can enjoy life more fully and completely. They will help you feel more motivated, too, as fatigue fuels apathy. Energy also makes you feel more invincible and more resilient. The lows in life don't seem so low and the highs last longer. You will have more humour to get you through the tough times and to enjoy the good times more fully. You will be more able to turn adversity into opportunity.

Select three techniques from this book that you think will make the biggest difference to you. Be aware that sometimes we feel resistance to what we need rather than what we want, so reflect on your reaction to each option and be curious about it. Ask what the reaction is about.

Then work your chosen techniques until they become habits. The work of Maxwell Maltz revealed that a habit takes at least 21 days to become ingrained. He was a plastic surgeon whose patients took 21 days to get used to their new face or to stop feeling their phantom limb after its removal. He observed within himself that it took him 21 days to form a new habit he wanted to cultivate. A study by Phillippa Lally, a health psychology researcher at University College London, suggests it takes even longer – an average of 66 days, depending on the complexity of the habit, the person and the circumstances. In her research the range was between 18 and 254 days.

While it is clear that everyone is different, you will *get* the results you want if you are persistent. If you are consistent, you will *keep* the results you want. That's the simple truth of it. There are no shortcuts. You are in charge of you. You get to make all the decisions about how you want your life to be, the director of your own life story.

To help you with your decisions, let me share with you my Five Principles of Change, shown here.

## THE FIVE PRINCIPLES OF CHANGE

1. **You have one life.** You can either fulfil your goals or live with regret.

2. **You have free will and response-ability.** You are not hostage to your desires – you have the power of choice.

3. **The most important thing you ever do is decide what's important.** Is it your long-term goal or satisfying this short-term desire?

**4. All choices have consequences.** Be honest with yourself about the consequences of your choices before making your decision.

**5. You are either moving towards or away from your goals.** Do you want to set yourself back or move yourself forward?

Another truth is that you are human. You are bound to slip from time to time. That's OK. You just need to get back on track. Remember that new habits are a process. Put in the work and you'll get the results.

If you are serious about change, treat your body like a bank account. You are constantly making deposits and withdrawals. For consistent energy, you need to make more deposits than withdrawals so that you have enough to draw on when the going gets tough. And when you want to enjoy life to the full, you'll have the energy for that, too.

Louise Hay, one of the first people to write about the connection between mind and body and the emotional causes of physical illness, identifies fatigue as 'resistance, boredom, lack of love for what one does'. Finding your enthusiasm for life, in whatever way works for you, can be enough to transform your energy. In my experience of working with clients, it is a significant factor, but not the only one. It is a complex picture and there is no one-size-fits-all approach.

This book will help you identify what might work for you. If you are in any doubt at all, do see a specialist. Life's too important to sleepwalk your way through it, don't you think?

## The Five Pillars and the Five Foundations

My work is based on the Five Pillars, which are the psychological, emotional, physical, lifestyle and spiritual aspects of life, as shown here.

| THE FIVE PILLARS | | |
|---|---|---|
| **Psychological** | Thoughts | Your behavioural response to stress |
| **Emotional** | Feelings | Your emotional response to stress |
| **Physical** | Nutrition and biochemistry | Your physical response to stress |
| **Lifestyle** | Life load | How your lifestyle contributes to stress |
| **Spiritual** | Purpose and meaning | Your ability to transcend negative stress |

These, in turn, give you the Five Foundations:

- Clarity
- Skills
- Confidence
- Health
- Energy

While energy is one of the Foundations, it is really a function of the Five Pillars.

By managing yourself, balancing all areas of your life, taking care of and responding to your body's needs and making sure you have a sense of purpose, you can expect to enjoy sustainable energy, a calm energy, a positive energy that enriches your life. There are other benefits to this: you will be less stressed, easier to be around, more productive and you won't take yourself so seriously. As someone once said, life is too important to take it seriously. We tend to make the small things the big things and overlook what really matters.

Don't let your burnout lead to your breakdown. Take steps now to build sustainable energy so you feel more motivated, more invincible, easily navigating any low points with the energy and mindset to enjoy the good times.

As a final, fun tip, if you suffer from driver's fatigue or need a quick boost, there is one thing that is great for keeping you awake – singing. Try it! It's fun, especially if you are singing along to something upbeat. It might get you a few strange looks but it's a great energizer and lifts your mood like nothing else.

······

# APPENDIX I

## The emotional freedom technique (EFT)

I came across this technique years ago, when it was new and many therapists I know were talking about it. At first, I thought it was hokum. But I kept hearing about it and eventually decided to give it a try. What a revelation. It is definitely weird but it is definitely wonderful. I now teach it to many of my clients as a way of managing their state.

A form of energy psychology, EFT is easy to learn but probably not so easy off the page. I do have a demonstration video and script builder, available at www.self-help-resources.co.uk and I will supplement that with some instructions here.

EFT is an energy therapy that works on the meridians of the body. These are the invisible energy channels we all have, similar to the blood vessels but not visible to the naked eye. They transport energy around the body and affect our emotions and physiology.

The principle is that negative emotion is caused by an interruption in the energy flow of the body. EFT serves to kick-start that energy and neutralize any negativity by a process of tapping meridian points while repeating a particular phrase. This is not to condone someone else's behaviour, nor is it so that you become a doormat or victim of external events. What it does is neutralize your relationship to what has happened and how you feel so that you feel more grounded, balanced and capable.

EFT can be used in three ways:

- To prepare for an event
- To reduce negative emotion after an event
- As daily maintenance for general wellbeing

It also helps to produce a calm, resourceful energy.

## DISCLAIMER

Because EFT can, on occasion, bring up deep and unresolved issues requiring the help of a trained therapist, these instructions are suitable only for people with everyday problems with minor emotional impact. If you suspect some deep-rooted trauma or if you think you may have, or have been diagnosed with, a psychological condition, it is better to work with a qualified therapist. If you are in any doubt, please do not use this process in any way that you feel might uncover areas that could cause adverse reactions of any kind. You are required to take complete responsibility for your own emotional and/or physical wellbeing.

# Getting started with EFT

There are two main components to EFT. First are the tapping points. Second is the phrase you need to repeat when tapping those points (the declaration phrase)

**STEP 1: THE TAPPING POINTS**
You will be tapping on the meridian points in the body. These points are used in acupuncture and, though we are not using needles, you need to make sure you are tapping in the right place. Here they are:

**1.** The side of your hand (the part you would use if you were doing a **karate chop**) – use the tips of your fingers against this part of your hand.

**2.** The **crown** of the head – use the flat of your hand on the crown of your head

**3.** At the inner corner of the **eyebrows** – use the tip of two of your fingers for this.

**4.** At the outside corner of the eyes (the bony part) (**side of eye**) – again, use the tip of two of your fingers.

**5.** On the bone about 1 cm (½ inch) below the pupil of the eyes. (**under eye**) – use the tip of two of your fingers.

**6.** Just **under the nose** in the centre – use the tip of two of your fingers.

**7.** Just below the lower lip in the centre of the face (**chin**) – use the tip of two of your fingers.

**8.** Just under the **collarbone** – use the flat of your hand on your chest and capture both of your collarbones as you do it.

**9. Under the arm** about 10 cm (4 inches) below the armpit – use the flat of your hand.

### STEP 2: IDENTIFY YOUR DISCOMFORT LEVEL

Now you know where to tap, determine the emotion you want to bring down and the level of your discomfort, with 10 being the worst that you can feel and 0 being perfect. For example, 'Out of 10, how anxious am I right now?' or 'Out of 10, how angry am I right now?'

The technique is intended to bring down this level of discomfort so that you feel more resourceful. Remember, it doesn't take the problem away; it just changes your relationship with it. It gives you a calmer energy so you can deal with it effectively. It isn't about letting people get away with anything. Nor is it about becoming aggressively assertive. It is about dealing with situations effectively, or neutralizing the negative emotion surrounding something.

## STEP 3: CHOOSE YOUR DECLARATION PHRASE

Establish a suitable and specific phrase that describes how you feel about the issue or emotion. This declaration phrase works best if you have the emotion you feel contained in the phrase. You are not looking for an affirmation here but a brief description of the emotion and the problem. Examples are:

- 'I'm angry with my sister for being late again.'
- 'I'm anxious about doing the presentation today.'
- 'I feel so confused about which to choose.'
- 'I soooo crave this chocolate now.'

The quality of the phrase you choose is key to the success of the process. The more specific the phrase, the more effective it will be, although it doesn't have to read like a legal document. Nor does it have to be suitable for a family audience or even grammatically correct. But it does have to *feel* right.

A mistake some people make is to make it an affirmation, such as 'I am going to have a nice time.' This just doesn't work. If you are worried you might not have a nice time, work on the emotion you experience that is preventing you from having one; for example, 'I am dreading going to the party.' If you reduce the dread, you are more likely to have a nice time.

## STEP 4: ADD A SET-UP PHRASE

Now add to your declaration phrase a phrase of self-acceptance. This is the set-up phrase. It is interesting how many people struggle to say this, which is why it is so powerful. It might go like this: 'Even though [your declaration phrase], I fully and completely accept myself without judgement.' Alternatives are: 'I deeply and completely accept/forgive/respect/love myself', etc., or any combination of these. The declaration must always *feel* right to you, even though you might not believe it at this point.

Here are some examples from the phrases used above:

- *Even though* I'm angry with my sister for being late again [declaration phrase], *I fully and completely accept myself without judgement.*

- *Even though* I'm anxious about doing the presentation today [declaration phrase], *I fully and completely accept myself without judgement.*

- *Even though* I feel so confused about which to choose [declaration phrase], *I fully and completely accept myself without judgement.*

- *Even though* I soooo crave this chocolate now [declaration phrase], *I fully and completely accept myself without judgement.*

### STEP 5: GO THROUGH THE PROCESS

**1. Set up:** Hold one hand flat, palm upwards, and with the fleshy side of the other hand 'chop' down onto the palm about seven times (**karate chop**) while repeating your whole phrase (declaration and set-up phrase). Repeat the phrase and the tapping three times in quick succession with as much belief and passion as possible. Faking it is fine, but you do need to have positive intent.

2. Tap about seven times on each meridian point as you repeat the issue or emotion once, as follows:

- the crown of the head
- the inner corner of the eyebrows
- the outside corner of the eyes (bony part) (side of eye)
- on the bone about 1 cm (½ inch) below the pupil of the eyes (under eye)
- just under the nose in the centre of the face
- just below the lower lip in the centre of the face (chin)
- with a flat hand just under the collarbone
- with a flat hand under the arm about 10 cm (4 inches) below the armpit
- chop down with the hand, as in 1 above (karate chop point)

3. Close your eyes, take a deep breath. Hold to the count of four and exhale to the count of eight.

4. Check your number (discomfort level) again. Repeat the whole process until you get a zero or as low as you would like the number to be. If it isn't coming down satisfactorily, change the declaration and try to be more specific. Remem-

ber, EFT is not about affirmations but about tapping out the negative emotion. You can also change the declaration as you go along, according to how you feel. For example, it might become 'the remnants of anger' or 'this slight anxiety'. Feel free to work with whatever comes up for you. Persistence and repetition will yield the best results.

**5.** Once you have cleared out the negative emotions (when the discomfort levels are close to or at zero), you can finish with a positive choice phrase such as 'I choose to feel calm and relaxed' or 'I choose to feel calm and resourceful', tapping on all the points as before. It is best to use this positive phrase only when you have cleared out any negativity; otherwise a small trigger will send you back to where you were before.

Now, you may spot that this technique would be unusual to watch. You'd be amazed how many people use it these days, and it is particularly popular with actors and performers, as well as people in business, stressed parents and people suffering from cravings.

### SUMMARY

For your convenience, here is a summary of the technique:

**1.** Choose an appropriate declaration phrase.
**2.** Assess your discomfort level out of 10.

**3.** Tap:

Karate Chop: *Even though* [declaration phrase], *I fully and completely accept myself without judgement x 3*

Crown: declaration phrase x 1
Eyebrow: declaration phrase x 1
Side of eye: declaration phrase x 1
Under eye: declaration phrase x 1
Under nose: declaration phrase x 1
Chin: declaration phrase x 1
Collarbone: declaration phrase x 1
Underarm: declaration phrase x 1
Karate chop: declaration phrase x 1

**4.** Breathe in deeply. Hold for a count of four and breathe out for a count of eight.

Repeat steps 1 to 4 until your discomfort is as low as you would like it.

Now tap on all the points with your chosen phrase.

For a personal script-builder and a video demonstration of EFT, please see www.self-help-resources.co.uk

・ ・ ・ ・ ・ ・

# APPENDIX II

## Know your alkaline-forming foods

Having too much acidity in your body can reduce your energy, cause illness and upset your digestion. The level of acidity is affected by the foods you eat, the amount you exercise and your mood. It is recommended that, for health, around 80 per cent of the food you eat should be alkaline-forming, with the remaining 20 per cent acid-forming. However, it's important to know that acid-forming foods are not always foods with an acidic flavour. For example, although a lemon has an acidic flavour it is alkaline-forming in the body. A good way to start your day is to have a glass of hot water with lemon in it.

The symptoms of excess acidity may include fatigue, irritability, sensitivity, aches/pains, headaches, insomnia, stomach acidity, acid reflux, indigestion and heartburn. The benefits of a more alkaline diet include improved heart function, reduced food cravings and greater emotional wellbeing.

Acid-forming foods are those rich in chlorine, phosphorus, sulphur and nitrogen. Alkaline-forming foods are those rich in calcium, magnesium, potassium and sodium. Here is a list of acid-forming and alkaline-forming foods:

**ALKALINE-FORMING FOODS**

Take 80 per cent of your food from this list.

| | | | |
|---|---|---|---|
| Avocado | Cider vinegar | Millet | Raspberries |
| Apricots | Coconut | Milk | Root vegetables |
| Apples | Dried fruit | Mushrooms | Seeds |
| Bananas | Figs | Onion | Peaches |
| Beans | Grapefruit | Oranges | Short-grain |
| Beetroot | Grapes | Potatoes | brown rice |
| Berries | Lemon | Peaches | Spinach |
| Cherries | Lentils | Pears | Tangerines |
| Cabbage | Linseeds | Prunes | Tomatoes |
| Carrots | Lettuce | Rhubarb | Yogurt |
| Celery | Melon | Quinoa | |

Also alkaline-forming:

- Deep breathing
- Skin brushing
- Hot water and lemon
- Yoga

**ACID-FORMING FOODS**

Take 20 per cent of your food from this list.

| | | | |
|---|---|---|---|
| Asparagus | Eggs | Mustard and cress | Sugar |
| Bacon | Fats | Olives | Stilton |
| Beef | Fizzy water | Oatmeal | Tapioca |
| Brazil nuts | Fried foods | Oats | Tea |

| | | | |
|---|---|---|---|
| Cheddar cheese | Hazelnuts | Plums | Veal |
| Chicken | Herrings | Rice | Walnuts |
| Coffee | Lamb | Rye | Wholemeal flour |
| Cola | Liver | Sago | Wheat |
| Cranberries | Mackerel | Salt | |
| Edam | Mayonnaise | Shellfish | |

Also acid-forming:

- Anger
- Negative emotions
- Smoking
- Excessive exercise

# •••••• 
# APPENDIX III

## Resources

Here is a list of recommended reading and other resources to help deepen your understanding of some of the concepts included in this book:

Batmanghelidj, F., *Your Body's Many Cries for Water* (Global Health Solutions, 2008)

Charvet, Shelle Rose, *Words That Change Minds* (Kendal Hunt, 2010)

Cloud, Henry and Townsend, John, *Boundaries* (Zondervan, 2002)

Cousins, Norman, *Anatomy of an Illness* (W.W. Norton, 2005)

Covey, Stephen R., *The 7 Habits of Highly Effective People* (Simon & Schuster, 2004)

Eden, Donna, *Energy Medicine* (Piatkus, 2008)

Emerald, David, *The Power of TED (The Empowerment Dynamic)* (Polaris, 2016)

Emoto, Masaru, *The Miracle of Water* (Atria, 2011)

Gilleman, Ann Louise, *Zapped* (HarperOne, 2011)

Gladwell, Malcolm, *Outliers: The Story of Success* (Penguin, 2009)

Greenblatt, Edy, *Restore Yourself: The Antidote for Professional Exhaustion* (Execu-Care, 2009)

Hamilton, David R., *Why Kindness is Good for You* (Hay House, 2010)

Harris, Thomas A., *I'm OK – You're OK* (Arrow, 1995)

Hay, Louise L. *Heal Your Body A-Z* (Hay House, 2004)

Hawkins, David, *Truth vs Falsehood* (Veritas, 2005)

Holford, Patrick, *The Low-GL Diet Bible* (Piatkus, 2009)

Holford, Patrick, *The Optimum Nutrition Bible* (Piatkus, 2004)

Karpman, Stephen B., *A Game Free Life* (Drama Triangle Publications, 2014)

Katie, Byron, *Loving What Is* (Rider, 2002)

Kingston, Karen, *Clear Your Cutter with Feng Shui* (Piatkus, 1998)

McDermott, Ian and O'Connor, Joseph, *Practical NLP for Managers* (Gower, 1996)

Weil, Andrew, *Eating Well for Optimum Health* (Sphere, 2008)

Woolfrey, Tricia and Craven, Helen, *An Inside Job*™ (www.triciawoolfrey.com)

Woolfrey, Tricia *Meal Planner* (www.triciawoolfrey.com)

Woolfrey, Tricia, *21 Ways and 21 Days to the Life You Want* (Verity, 2008)

Woolfrey, Tricia, *Sleep Well* MP3 (www.triciawoolfrey.com)

Woolfrey, Tricia, *Think Positive, Feel Good* (Verity, 2008)

Young, Robert O., *The pH Miracle* (Piatkus, 2009)